Married for Life

Life-giving principles that make a marriage last

Revised 2001

The Couples' Home Group Ministry of

Official Curriculum of

Copyright © 1986-2001 by: Mike and Marilyn Phillipps.

ISBN 1-884794-02-5

Printed in U.S.A.

Revised 2001

All rights reserved. Written permission must be secured from the publishers to utilize any part of this book for any purpose other than the conducting of authorized Marriage Ministries International groups.

Published by:	Eden Publishing
In Cooperation With:	Marriage Ministries International, Inc. PO Box 1040 Littleton, CO 80160-1040 USA

    Scripture quotations marked (NIV) are from the Holy Bible, New International Version. Copyright © 1973, 1978, 1984, International Bible Society. Used by permission.
    Scripture taken from the AMPLIFIED BIBLE, Old Testament. Copyright © 1962, 1964 by Zondervan Publishing House. Used by permission.
    Scripture taken from the AMPLIFIED BIBLE, New Testament. Copyright © 1954, 1958 by the Lockman Foundation. Used by permission.
    Scriptures taken from The New King James Version. Copyright © 1979, 1980, 1982, Thomas Nelson Inc., Publishers. Used by permission.

PREFACE

Welcome to Married for Life!*

Ever since God healed our "impossible" marriage several years ago, it has been the desire of our hearts to share with other couples the healing and restorative power of God's Word. The Bible not only contains the prescription for the healing of broken marriages, it is also the source of God's vision and blueprint for all marriages. **Married for Life** is enabling couples across our nation and around the world to be reached with this exciting news concerning marriage.

When we marry, we are called of God into the office of husband and wife. It is His anointing that enables us to fulfill the call as He directs. Marriage was intended by God to be a vibrant, dynamic state of ever-deepening love and growth. With God's direction we can truly go from "glory to glory" in our life together as husband and wife. **Married for Life** is recapturing God's heart for His people in an area in which the world has totally lost the vision - marriage. An army of couples is emerging around the world—couples with God's vision in their hearts and His weapons in their hands—couples who know victory in Jesus and are prepared to share it with others. Marriages have been under attack for long enough. Now they are becoming a powerful offensive force. Come, join the ranks!

With grateful hearts to Jesus,

Mike & Marilyn

Mike and Marilyn Phillipps
Founding Directors
Marriage Ministries International, Inc

---

*The couples' home group ministry of Marriage Ministries International.

Acknowledgments:

We would like to take this opportunity to gratefully acknowledge all those who have helped in the formation of **Married for Life**. They have helped us preserve the vision of Marriage Ministries International with unwavering faith and have been instrumental in seeing that vision come to pass. Their encouragement has been invaluable.

We would like to thank all the Group Leaders who have shared their insights and revelations with us to expand and deepen these teachings. Their feedback has provided a very special dimension that would not have been possible without them.

And finally, we would like to thank each and every couple who has gone or is now going through a **Married for Life** group. Each of you are very precious to us. Your growth and transformation in Jesus is our greatest reward. It is your contribution of yourselves—your time, your enthusiasm, your love, and your financial resources—that enables us to bring to pass the vision that God gave. We love you all!

It Is Time to Rebuild The Wall

> So they said, "Let us rise up and build."
> Then they set their hands to do this good work."
> Nehemiah 2:18b

Read the book of Nehemiah in the Bible. You will see a story of a man called to rebuild the city walls of Jerusalem, walls that had been torn down and burned by their enemies. The task was an awesome one—almost an impossible one. There were many who opposed the work, many who ridiculed Nehemiah and those he rallied to rebuild.

The people were placed along the wall in families, each to rebuild their own section so that the city might once again be safe and protected. The families faced the constant threat of enemy attack. In fact, when the wall was halfway up, they began holding a weapon in one hand and working with the other. Not only were they totally devoted to the work of rebuilding but they also were fully committed to fighting off the enemy should it become necessary.

Today the wall of protection afforded by strong families in each of our cities has been destroyed by enemy attack. The disintegration of marriage and family through the past generations has left us vulnerable. Now each family must fight its own battles without the corporate protection afforded by a strong wall.

The time has come to rebuild that wall! Just as in the day of Nehemiah, God is appointing and anointing families to rally and restore the safety and security of the homes of our land.

In Nehemiah's day families stood side by side to rebuild, each at their appointed post, doing their portion of the work. Today it is also true that strong marriages and families bring strength to a city. Strong families provide corporate protection for our churches and our cities. Homes that are broken and in ruin leave our cities and the churches within them open and vulnerable to enemy attack.

The wall composed of strong families provides protection. **It is the Word of God, the Bible, that provides the blueprint for rebuilding that strong wall of protection.** When we use God's plan, His Word, as our blueprint and His tools, scriptural principles, we build a strong, healthy hedge of protection around our marriage and our home. Our children have a safe place in which to dwell.

The Word of God also provides boundaries, though, and as the standard that provides protection is raised, the boundaries it provides are also put in place. Many today want the protection but shun the boundaries. It is truly a time of each one doing what seems right in his own eyes.

©Marriage Ministries International

When we do our own thing, through either ignorance or self-will, **we refuse the boundaries of God's Word and consequently also lose its protection.** Our cities now reflect that rejection of God's plan in the destruction of homes and families. Just as Nehemiah observed in Nehemiah 2:14, the destruction is so great that in some places there is nothing but rubble.

Perhaps your own marriage is in rubble at this moment. Perhaps you feel like one of the burned stones that Sanballat said could never be used to build a strong wall [Nehemiah 4:2]. Nehemiah didn't listen to the voice of his enemy and neither should you. Jesus has great plans for you and wants to rebuild you in strength and might. As you submit to the blueprint of God's Word, accepting both His boundaries and His protection, your marriage and your home can be transformed by His power.

Or perhaps you only have a few cracks in your wall, small areas of erosion that are beginning to wear away. You recognize the need to strengthen your wall and fortify it using God's blueprint as your guide. There is no better time to begin rebuilding than when problems are first recognized. Your stones are not yet burned, your portion of the wall is not yet crumbled. Minor adjustments here and there will firmly establish your marriage on the Rock and solidify the protection of your wall.

If you now have a strong marriage, established and grounded in the Word, you have much to offer others. The strength and stability of your portion of the wall is vital to others. Many times it is hard to help others build or rebuild with any success, though, if you are not sure exactly how your portion of the wall became so strong. You need to know the blueprint you have followed so that you might share it with others. Knowing which tools from God's Word have established and strengthened your marriage will enable you to help others rebuild and strengthen their own homes and marriages.

Whatever the situation of your marriage and home today, you can be blessed and grow in the Lord through an understanding and application of His blueprint for your marriage and home. Nehemiah encouraged the people, *"Do not be afraid of them. Remember the Lord, great and awesome, and fight for your brethren, your sons, your daughters, your wives, and your homes"* [Nehemiah 4:14]. Perhaps not since then has the call to battle been more needed than today. The sound of the trumpet can be heard in the land [Nehemiah 4:20] and the Lord is saying, "Rebuild!"

Welcome to Married for Life! We recognize that we are part of the army that the Lord is raising up in this hour to rebuild and strengthen the home. Our constant prayer for you is that your home might become an oasis of peace to the hurting and a lighthouse to those lost in darkness. Make the most of these next fourteen weeks—for yourselves and for others who need encouragement as they take their places along the wall. One by one, as we link strong and fortified homes together in Christ, the protection and the boundaries of God will be evidenced in our cities and our churches. Whether your stones are burned and crumbled today or whether your walls are only slightly eroded, or whether you have a strong, fortified portion of the wall, we all need you. Be blessed and be a blessing!

Contents

THE VISION 2
ORGANIZATION 2
COMMITMENT 3
ORDER OF MEETINGS 4
PERMISSION TO SHARE WITH PASTORS 5
MMI CORE VALUES 7

LESSONS

COVENANT 8
ONE-FLESH 16
ROLES 26
SOWING AND REAPING 38
FORGIVENESS 46
FAITH VISION AND TRUST 54
PRAYING TOGETHER 64
AGREEMENT 72
FLOWING TOGETHER IN THE SPIRIT 80
INTIMACY 90
SPIRITUAL WARFARE 100
LIFE PATTERNS 110
ONE-FLESH MINISTRY 120
DESTINY IN PROGRESS 130

LIFE APPLICATION

COVENANT LIFE APPLICATION 133
ONE-FLESH LIFE APPLICATION 141
ROLES LIFE APPLICATION 145
SOWING AND REAPING LIFE APPLICATION 153
FORGIVENESS LIFE APPLICATION 162
FAITH VISION AND TRUST LIFE APPLICATION 166
PRAYING TOGETHER LIFE APPLICATION 169
AGREEMENT LIFE APPLICATION 173
FLOWING TOGETHER IN THE SPIRIT LIFE APPLICATION 176
INTIMACY LIFE APPLICATION 180
SPIRITUAL WARFARE LIFE APPLICATION 184
LIFE PATTERNS LIFE APPLICATION 188
ONE-FLESH MINISTRY LIFE APPLICATION 191

©Marriage Ministries International

THE VISION

We welcome you to your Married for Life group. We know you are going to be blessed here and that your marriage will never again be the same!

When God first shared His desire regarding the ministry of MMI, He expressed it in a vision of millions of twinkling lights around the world. There was one on every block, around every corner. God said that each one of those twinkling lights was a powerhouse Christian home where the peace and the power of the Lord so radiated that each one was an oasis to the thirsty world around them. God promised that He would raise them up around the world. These homes would be the product of godly couples seeking the Lord's will for their own one-flesh relationship and desiring to minister to others. They would be free of strife and endowed with power to tear down enemy strongholds, setting others free in Jesus' name.

Powerful one-flesh teams have now begun to cover the earth. Today is your day to begin transforming your home into a peaceful oasis for your neighborhood. During the next fourteen weeks you are going to be led of the Spirit into exciting new concepts for your marriage. You will learn what a true "one-flesh" relationship is and how to realize the fulfillment of that in your lives. You will acquire knowledge and wisdom that, when applied, will enable your home to be free from strife. Sowing and reaping peace, contentment and harmony will become a routine part of your married life. You will learn to effectively fight spiritual warfare on behalf of your spouse and your children. You will see lives drastically changed by the Word of God. And you will learn how to reproduce these miracles of God in the lives of others.

ORGANIZATION

Each Married for Life home group is composed of a maximum of seven couples. Leadership consists of a Group Leader couple and a Leader in Training couple. The group meets weekly for fourteen weeks and couples are asked to commit to the group for that period of time. After this time they may opt to continue again through the basic course, branch out into ministry, and/or continue on in deeper one-flesh teachings. The thirteenth week will provide couples with information regarding available one-flesh ministry opportunities.

The final week is an outreach night. This is your "graduation night" and you are encouraged to invite family and friends to attend. This is also an information night regarding Marriage Ministries International, so invite any and all couples you know who are interested in being in a Married for Life group. Couples **must** attend an outreach night if they wish to join a group. At the close of the outreach meeting, new couples will be given an opportunity to sign up and become part of the new group(s) that will be forming. Outreach night is the only night which couples outside the group may attend.

COMMITMENT

If it is your goal to operate together as one in peace and harmony and have your marriage be exactly what God has in mind for it, then you have come to the right place. If you are serious about this commitment, we ask you to commit to meeting for the next thirteen weeks with this Married for Life group. Do not take this commitment lightly. Consider the cost up front and when you commit to faithfulness, be faithful.

The first step in any change is a determined commitment to that purpose. We ask you to discuss this together as a couple and if this is where you believe God is calling you, we ask that you signify your commitment to God and each other by signing the following agreement. This is not a promise to us - but to each other and to our Father of your determination to seek His best. He is faithful! You are going to be amazed at what you see Him do.

Father,

We acknowledge that You recognize us as one-flesh. We want to know in a greater measure what this means. We want to live in peace and harmony using Your scriptural principles to accomplish this. We want our home to be an oasis of peace to Your glory. We commit today to pressing in diligently to acquire Your best for our marriage and home.

We lay aside all preconceived ideas, notions, and philosophies that we have regarding marriage, good or bad. We give you permission to work in our hearts whatever we need to grow in our relationship with You and with each other.

We agree also to respect the rights of the other couples who are in our group. We will keep confidential all that is shared here and will expect the same of others. We support others in their growth as one-flesh couples and desire to do nothing that would hinder that growth. We also agree to pray for the other couples in our group weekly.

_____ _____
Husband   Wife

_____
Date February 20, 2005

"Marriage Ministries International is a teaching ministry and offers no professional or clinical counseling. MMI does not present its staff or field leadership as medical or psychological experts capable of dealing with severe emotional or psychological disorders. MMI courses or materials are not intended as a substitute for professional or pastoral counseling."

ORDER OF MEETINGS

"Let all things be done decently and in order." 1 Corinthians 14:40

There will be quite a few of us in this room for the next few weeks, so we ask that the following guidelines be observed to maximize our time together:

1. We will meet once a week for approximately two to two-and-one-half hours. Please be punctual and plan to stay the entire time.

2. Please do not interrupt the teaching. If you have any questions during the teaching, please write them down and bring them up during the clarification period at the end of the teaching.

3. The Question and Answer period after the teaching is to clarify any point that may not have been clear or that you do not understand. It is not a time to debate what has been taught or to offer your opinion. If you disagree with the teaching, we ask that you search the Word with an open heart and see what the Spirit of God speaks to you. If after you do this you still disagree, contact your lead couple and ask to meet with them.

4. All that is shared here by couples is to be held in strictest confidence by the group.

5. No new couples may visit or join the group once the group has begun with the exception of City or Area Directors who may visit the group for purposes of administrative oversight.

6. All materials used or recommended here must first be approved by MMI International Headquarters in Colorado. This includes tapes and books. This group is not to be used by group members as a distribution area for handouts or any other materials.

7. All couples who commit to the group are asked to complete the entire fourteen weeks.

8. There are to be no children at Married for Life meetings. This includes babies.

9. No food is to be served at regular weekly meetings because this is a class, not a social gathering. Food is welcome the fourteenth week.

10. Meetings ARE NOT TO BE TAPED under any circumstances.

BEFORE YOUR BEGIN:

- ✍ FOR YOUR CONVENIENCE AN OUTLINE OF EACH LESSON IS LOCATED ON THE LEFT SIDE OF YOUR BOOK.

- ✍ THIS PROVIDES YOU WITH THE DETAILED INFORMATION FOR EACH LESSON SO YOU DO NOT HAVE TO TAKE IN-DEPTH NOTES AND CAN LISTEN TO THE TEACHING.

- ✍ THE LESSON WILL BE PRESENTED IN THE ORDER OF YOUR OUTLINE SO THAT YOU CAN FOLLOW ALONG.

- ✍ ON THE RIGHT SIDE A NOTE-TAKING AREA IS PROVIDED FOR YOU.

PERMISSION TO SHARE WITH PASTOR

What couples share in groups is confidential and is not to be shared outside the group. Sometimes, however, pastors ask MMI leaders how couples in their church are doing in their group. We believe that the role of your pastor is extremely important in your life and want to complement the work of your local church. Should your pastor ask regarding you and your marriage, we need to know your feelings regarding the sharing of information.

Please indicate below what your desires are regarding sharing information with your pastor and give that section to your leaders. We appreciate you letting us know your wishes.

-- ✂

We ☐ do ☐ do not give you permission to share with our pastor regarding our participation in this Married for Life group should you be asked. Our pastor's name is

_____ at _____

church.

_____   _____
            Husband   Wife

Date _____

THE CORE VALUES OF
MARRIAGE MINISTRIES INTERNATIONAL

These are the principles upon which the ministry is based.

- ➢ Are unchangeable
- ➢ Determine the form and the flow of ministry
- ➢ Determine what is negotiable and what is not
- ➢ Help people identify their call
- ➢ Are the basis for reproducibility

MARRIAGE MINISTRIES INTERNATIONAL'S CORE VALUES

1. Everything we do must point people to the Lordship of Jesus.
    - ➢ Jesus is the only way to the Father and to eternal life.
2. Powerhouse homes flow in the power of the Holy Spirit.
    - ➢ The power of the Holy Spirit changes the believer from within and then flows outward to others.
3. Marriage is a covenant relationship.
    - ➢ Marriage relationship and commitment is to reflect the Lord's covenant relationship with His Church.
4. Marriage between a man and a woman is the basis for God's plan for family.
    - ➢ God established marriage in the Garden of Eden with a man and a woman and gave us His blueprint.
5. We are to make disciples of all nations.
    - ➢ Discipling is based in relationship and includes training, modeling, and accountability.
6. We are to produce fruit with the seed of reproducibility.
    - ➢ Our goal is not to make others dependent on us but rather teach them to develop a deepening relationship with the Lord and reach out to others in His name.
7. When a couple marries, their individual call and destiny are blended together.
    - ➢ The synergism of one-flesh enables a couple to accomplish far more than they ever could alone.
8. Homes are points of out-reach to a lost world.
    - ➢ MMI groups meet in homes to remind us that God desires to reach our neighborhoods from our homes, lighthouses shining in the darkness.
9. God views families generationally.
    - ➢ The decisions we make today affect the families of tomorrow.
10. We are an army.
    - ➢ We need to be obedient to the directions of the Lord for our lives, going where He says to go and doing what He says to do.

A. Understanding Covenant
1. The true weight of covenant agreement
   a. Contract = limited liability
   b. Covenant = unlimited liability
      1) …strong commitment--loyalty unto death.
      2) …death to independent living.
   c. Covenant partners lay down their lives for each other.
      1) Each individual life is no longer the priority.
      2) The life shared between them becomes their priority.
2. Components of a Covenant
   a. Promises ~
      1) Express interpersonal commitment.
      2) Pledge of the partners' fidelity in keeping the covenant.
      3) Indicate what they will do.
   b. Terms ~
      1) Indicate conditions under which the agreement will be fulfilled.
      2) Indicate the duration of the covenant.
      3) May or may not be accompanied by an oath.

B. Types of Covenants
1. God-Man Covenants
   a. Eight covenants between God and man are recorded in the Bible.
      1) Revealed God's perfect will and purpose for man [Psalm 111].
      2) Reflected God's love, grace and mercy.
      3) Revealed God as a covenant-keeper as well as a covenant-maker [Isaiah 54:10, Psalm 89:34].
   b. God is faithful even though man may not be.
   c. God enables man to keep covenants [2 Timothy 1:12; 2 Corinthians 3:4-6].
2. Man-Man Covenants.
   a. Made to bind each other to the relationship.
   b. Covenant partners are dedicated to the relationship and to ensuring its continuation.
   c. Partners exchange all they possess [1 Samuel 18:1-4].
      1) Jonathan gave David:
         a) Cloak (symbol of wealth).
         b) Garments (symbol of all his possessions).
         c) Sword (symbol of strength).
         d) Belt (symbol of protection—covering life-giving parts).
      2) All are representative of what is exchanged in a man-man covenant.

Personal Application

Special Scriptures

COVENANT

C. Marriage as a Covenant.
1. Scripture indicates marriage is a covenant.
   a. Malachi 2:14 NIV (to the man) *"...it is because the Lord is acting as the witness between you and the wife of your youth, because you have broken faith with her, though she is your partner, the wife of your marriage covenant."*
   b. Proverbs 2:17 NIV (to the woman) *"...who has left the partner of her youth and ignored the covenant she made before God."*
   c. *"What God has joined together"* is a description of the two being made into one [Matthew 19:6; Genesis 2:24].
      1) Only God can make two into one.
         a) When a couple chooses to marry, they are joined together in God's plan of unity called marriage.
         b) *"Joined together"* is the making into one.
      2) Without God, marriage is only a man-man covenant.
         a) The couple *is* married.
         b) God does not live within either partner and so He is a witness but not an active partner in the marriage.
   d. God expects us to even honor covenants that are not of His choosing.
      1) Joshua 9 and 10
         a) Israelites instructed to destroy enemies in Promised Land.
         b) Gibeonites feared Israelites and pretended to come from a far away land.
         c) Israelites did not seek God and made covenant with them.
         d) Even required to go to war to protect covenant partners.
      2) 2 Samuel 21:1-6
         a) David inquired of God regarding three-year famine in land.
         b) Caused by Saul's household killing the Gibeonites.
         c) Gibeonites allowed to seek revenge on Saul's household.
         d) Famine ended.
2. Marriage Covenant.
   a. Promises.
      1) We made certain promises to each other on our wedding day.
      2) (Love, honor, cherish, obey, etc.).
   b. Terms.
      1) We agreed to certain terms on our wedding day.
      2) (For better or for worse, till death do us part).
   c. As covenant partners, we exchanged all we had previously held separately.
      1) 1 Corinthians 7:4 tells us we exchange our bodies.
      2) All goods are now also held in common.
      3) All of our wealth and all our debts are shared in common.
      4) Our strengths are pooled for our mutual protection.
      5) Strife can result from retaining possessions as "mine" not "ours."
         a) "My" salary, "your" debt.
         b) Gifts and inheritances may wrongly be seen as exclusively belonging to one and not the other.

WEEK 1

PERSONAL APPLICATION

SPECIAL SCRIPTURES

COVENANT

    d. Stepchildren are also included in our exchange.
        1) They belong to the stepparent as much as to the natural parent.
            a) Lack of understanding this principle sets the family up for strife and rebellion.
            b) Strife gives the children power to separate parents.
        2) Jesus is their example.
            a) Luke 2:51 says He submitted Himself to **them**--both parents.
            b) Mary was His natural parent, Joseph was His stepparent.
        3) Children must honor and obey their stepparent in the same manner as their natural parent.
3. Covenant is death to independent living.
    a. No longer "me" but now "we."
    b. Each spouse can hold the other accountable to the covenant promises he or she made [Jeremiah 3:14; Numbers 30:2].
4. Marriage covenant is sealed with vows [Ecclesiastes 5:4,5].
    a. Ecclesiastes 5:4,5 says it is better not to vow at all than to vow and not keep our word.
    b. Marriage vows are a serious matter.

D. Marriage in Christ as a Double Covenant.
    1. God instituted marriage in Garden of Eden as first man-man covenant [Genesis 2:24].
        a. God intended to be part of marriage from the beginning.
        b. God's initial covenant with man was tied to original marriage of man and woman [Genesis 1:27,28].
        c. When God is in the marriage covenant it is a God-man and man-man covenant.
    2. Benefits of marriage covenant as God intended marriage to be are therefore available only to those in covenant with God [Jeremiah 32:38-41].
    3. Who is in covenant with God?
        a. God covenanted with several people in a progressive pattern in the Old Testament.
        b. After Abraham, only the Jews were in covenant with God and people had to become Jews to enter into His covenant.
        c. Gentiles were permitted covenant relationship only after they were grafted in [Romans 11:13-21].
        d. Now the only way to enter into covenant with God is through Jesus.
            1) John 14:6; 1 John 2:23; John 15:23.
            2) Without Jesus, "...all our righteous acts are like filthy rags" [Isaiah 64:6].
            3) God does not recognize covenant benefits for the unsaved [Ephesians 2:12,13 Amplified].
            4) Jesus paid the price for us to be able to enter into covenant with God and He is the ONLY way to the Father now [John 14:6].

Week 1

Personal Application

Special Scriptures

COVENANT

4. How God becomes part of the marriage covenant.
    a. God witnesses our marriage on our wedding day, [Malachi 2:14] but if neither partner is saved, God is not an active part of the marriage.
    b. When at least one of the marriage partners receives Jesus, God becomes a covenant partner in the marriage [1 Corinthians 7:14 Amplified].
        1) The unbelieving partner is sanctified (set apart) by believer's relationship with God.
        2) The unbelieving partner receives covenant benefits through prayers of the believing spouse.
    c. Each spouse must make a personal commitment to Jesus to receive salvation [Romans 3:22-24].
        1) 1 Corinthians 7:16 is not a discouragement.
        2) Trust God to use whom He will to bring your spouse to salvation.
        3) You may not be the one who does it.
5. When both partners are redeemed in Jesus, the marriage is then able to move into the fullness of one-flesh as God intended marriage to be.
    a. God is in covenant with each partner through the New Covenant of Jesus.
    b. Couple is covenanted together in marriage according to the plan of God.
    c. Couple is now redeemed back to all that God intended when He first instituted marriage.
    d. They now have the potential for the unity God intended [Ecclesiastes 4:9-12].
    e. They now have the potential for the power God intended [Leviticus 26:8].
    f. Once both marriage partners are in Christ, they are ready to mature through God's blueprint for marriage [Jeremiah 32:38-41].

WEEK 1

PERSONAL APPLICATION

SPECIAL SCRIPTURES

A. The Creation of One-Flesh.
1. An understanding of one-flesh is found in Genesis 1 and 2.
   a. Adam was made in the image of God [Genesis 1:27].
   b. Adam was complete and whole, containing within one person all the attributes we now know as male and female [Genesis 1:27; Genesis 5:2].
   c. God removed a rib ("*chamber*" in Hebrew, indicating capacity) from Adam and formed woman that Adam named Eve [Genesis 2:21,22; Genesis 3:20].
   d. God referred to the two who became one as "Adam" [Genesis 5:2].
2. Adam and Eve created to be complementary and completing to each other.
   a. Each was created to fulfill and complete the other.
      1) Genesis 2:18 said Eve was to be an aid or helper suitable to Adam.
         a) King James uses the word *meet* for suitable.
         b) Hebrew word for helper comes from the root that means to "surround."
      2) Because they had the nature of God, it was their nature to love and to give [Genesis 1:26].
   b. The result of two people giving actively to each other, preferring each other totally is the wholeness of one-flesh as God intended it to be.
      1) They strengthened each other and were stronger together than either of them were individually.

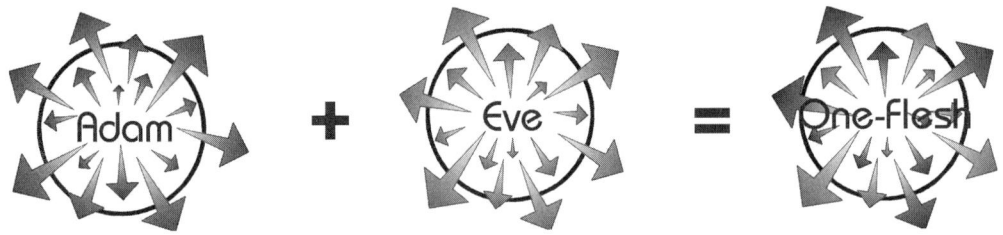

      2) *"Therefore shall a man leave his father and his mother, and shall cleave unto his wife: and they shall be one flesh"* [Genesis 2:24 KJV]. (Cleaving is an active, purposeful positioning and it means "to adhere, be joined together, to catch by pursuit.")
   c. God established synergism in one-flesh.
      1) Synergism means the whole is greater than the sum of the parts.
      2) Each had unique qualities and attributes which enhanced their unity.
      3) They combined the same qualities as Adam had alone, but by God's design their combined power and ability were greater [Leviticus 26:8].
         a) Alone—God had Adam just cultivate and keep the Garden [Genesis 2:15].
         b) Together—Adam and Eve, were *"...to fill the earth, subdue it, and rule over...every living thing"* [Genesis 1:28 NIV].

Personal Application

Special Scriptures

1 + 1 = far more than 2

ONE-FLESH

3. Meaning of one-flesh [Genesis 2:23-25].
   a. One-flesh is a benefit of covenant [Genesis 2:24].
   b. We are a 3-part being [1 Thessalonians 5:23].
   c. Adam and Eve had total unity of their three-part beings: Spirit, Soul, and Body.
   d. Our goal is total unity of the three.
      1) Body (flesh).
         a) Physical one-flesh unity is easiest for us to understand.
         b) *"And they shall be one flesh"* [Genesis 2:24 NKJV]. *"Be fruitful and multiply"* [Genesis 1:28 NKJV].
      2) Soul (intellect, emotions, will).
         a) This is hardest to achieve.
         b) They *"...were not ashamed"* [Genesis 2:25]. (Hebrew word for "ashamed" is translated in other parts of Old Testament as "confused".)
         c) For there to have been no confusion between them, they must have had total agreement in the soul realm.
      3) Spirit.
         a) Both Adam and Eve were created in the image of God and therefore had the unity of His Spirit.
         b) *"Did He not create a single being that has flesh and breath of life (spirit) ...Be careful of your own life, therefore, and do not break faith with the wife of your youth"* [Malachi 2:15 Jerusalem Bible].
         c) *"Has not the Lord made them one? In flesh and spirit they are His."* [Malachi 2:15 NIV].
         d) As members of the Body of Christ, are automatically one in Spirit.
   e. At the time of marriage, a one-flesh relationship comes into being.
      1) It must be nurtured and nourished to mature.
      ★ 2) We need to honor and esteem the needs of our covenant partner above our own.
      3) Philippians 2:3-4 NKJV, *"Let each of you look out not only for his own interests..."* As we place the needs of our spouse above our own, we nurture our one-flesh relationship and are blessed.
   f. Genesis 2:25 contains revelation concerning God's plan and potential for our one-flesh lives as husband and wife.
      1) They were married, man and wife. (Genesis 2:24 is the covenant verse-leaving in order to cleave.)
      2) "Both" indicates equality before God (also Galatians 3:28).
      3) No shame or darkness (sin) between them. Imagine being totally naked, in all ways—physically, emotionally, and spiritually, with your spouse with no shame—no confusion!
      4) "Transparent" in spirit, soul and body; free to be themselves, openly and honestly.
      5) This is God's plan for your marriage also.

WEEK 2

PERSONAL APPLICATION

SPECIAL SCRIPTURES

ONE-FLESH

B. The Fall [Genesis 3].
1. Satan recognized the unity and power in their relationship.
   a. He devised plan to use a quality placed within them by God to pit them against God and each other [vs. 6].
   b. Convinced Eve to fulfill herself [vs. 6].
   c. Adam followed and fulfilled his flesh despite what God had told him [Genesis 2:17].
2. They no longer had the nature of God and each began to fulfill self at the expense of the other.

   a. They covered themselves from each other [Genesis 3:7].
      1) "Self" is mentioned the first time in scripture after the fall.
      2) Were no longer transparent before each other.
      3) This pattern continues today as couples protect themselves and hide from each other.
   b. They hid from God [Genesis 3:8].
      1) Feared God and no longer saw Him as part of their marriage.
      2) Couples today fail to recognize that God must be the center and foundation of their marriage.
   c. They became confused as to whom their enemy was [Genesis 3:12].
      1) They failed to recognize Satan as their enemy and instead he blamed her and she blamed the serpent.
      2) Couples today are also tricked by the enemy into thinking that their spouse is the problem.
   d. They justified their sin and perpetuated the problem [Genesis 3:12].
      1) Failed to admit their fault in the sin.
      2) Couples today also justify sin instead of calling it sin and repenting.
3. Marriage deteriorated more as time passed.
   a. Of spirit, soul, and body, only physical unity was left [Genesis 4:1].
   b. Polygamy, multiple concubines, division, and divorce increased throughout the Old Testament.
   c. Finally Moses required a written divorce decree to keep matters straight [Matthew 5:31].

Personal Application

Why was he equally responsible?

Special Scriptures

Week 2

ONE-FLESH

C. Redemption in Jesus.
   1. Jesus came to redeem mankind back to original relationship with God that Adam had lost [Romans 5:18; 2 Corinthians 5:15].
   2. Jesus also redeemed for marriage what had been lost at the fall.
      [Galatians 3:13a says Christ redeemed us from the curse of the law. Curses about marriage and family are listed in Deuteronomy 28:30-32.]
   3. He renewed the original standards for marriage [Matthew 19:3-9; Mark 10:2-12; Luke 16:18].
      a. Pharisees tried to trap Jesus regarding the Mosaic Law [Matthew 19:7].
      b. Jesus did not clarify Mosaic Law.
      c. He used God's original plan for His point of reference.
      d. Divorce was permitted when hearts were hard.
         1) Hard hearts are a pre-redemption condition.
         2) Jesus came to change hardened hearts [Jeremiah 32:39; Ezekiel 11:19,20].
         3) The original plan of God did not include separation or divorce; *"...but from the beginning it was not so"* [Matthew 19:8 KJV].
      e. Jesus gave no excuse for divorce when He was talking privately to His disciples in Mark 10:10-12 and said that remarriage is adultery.
      f. **Divorce is not an option for Christians.**
      g. *"...except for sexual immorality..."* [Matthew 19:9], was spoken to hard-hearted Pharisees, not disciples. (It referred to the Jewish betrothal period and was clarification of Jewish law regarding sexual sin *before* marriage.)
      h. 1 Corinthians 7:11 gives us clear direction (remain single or be reconciled).
      i. **Remarriage while the former partner lives is an act of adultery.** [Romans 7:3, Luke 16:18, Mark 10:11,12].

D. No Condemnation [Romans 8:1-2].
   1. If you have experienced divorce and remarriage as a Christian:
      a. Regardless of how you came to these decisions, you need to search the Scriptures regarding God's standard for covenant.
      b. **This teaching is not meant to put you under condemnation!**
      c. When we discover that we have gone against God's will in any area of our life, we need to repent, receive forgiveness, and go on with God [1 John 1:9].
      d. It is better to recognize sin and repent than to defend our actions.
   2. Repenting.
      a. It is the act of remarriage, not the ongoing sexual union, that is adultery.
      b. When remarriage is adultery, the marriage is established on a sinful foundation; Jesus cannot enter into a sinful union.
      c. Repentance of the sinful basis of the marriage establishes it on Jesus as the foundation and opens the door for Him to be a vital part of the marriage.
      d. Please search the scriptures to determine their true meaning. Confusion arises when people's opinions are valued equally with the scriptures.
      e. The purpose of this teaching is to bring freedom and to end the harassment and condemnation that sin brings.

WEEK 2

PERSONAL APPLICATION

SPECIAL SCRIPTURES

Bassett

- God is perfect, he can't be wrong. If he is is then he is not Holy.

Pacman

3. Once you have repented and received God's forgiveness, do not allow the enemy to harass and condemn you anymore.
4. As your testimony lines up with the Word of God, you can help others avoid the pain and turmoil you have experienced.
5. Proceed from this point today and let the past go.

E. Marriage in Christ.
1. Only in Jesus can we receive all God has for marriage because He is the only One who has purchased back that which was lost through Adam and Eve.
2. Without Jesus, marriage can only be a counterfeit of what God intends.
3. We are born with selfish, inward-turned natures.
    a. This is why we must be born a second time [John 3:3].
    b. Without Jesus, we can only strive to improve ourselves with worldly techniques and methods.
    c. Only Jesus can change hearts.
    d. Marriage redeemed in Jesus need not conform to earthly standards nor be plagued by those things that are destroying marriages around us.

One-flesh

4. God has provided tools which enable us to construct our marriages on His blueprint for marriage.
5. When we have God's vision for marriage and use the principles of His Word, our homes become the oases of peace and power that God intends.

PERSONAL APPLICATION

Sin is sin. We all do it and we all need forgiveness.
I forget to forgive myself.

SPECIAL SCRIPTURES

A. God's Pattern for Roles.

  1. Creation.
     a. Genesis 1:26.
        1) God created Adam in His image.
        2) Adam was whole and complete.
     b. Genesis 2:22.
        1) Eve was taken from Adam, not formed separately.
        2) Each one retained qualities that the other needed.
     c. Man and woman were created to be complementary, not competing.

  2. After the fall, it was no longer possible to discern God's plan for marriage by observing earthly couples.
     a. In Ephesians 5:22-33, God gave example for marriage based on the relationship of Christ, the Bridegroom, and the Church, His Bride.
     b. Roles of husband and wife can be understood by observing Jesus' and the Church's interaction.

B. Jesus/husband and Church/wife roles:

  1. This is not intended to compare the redemptive role of Jesus.

  2. Some roles are the same for both husband and wife.

  3. This lesson is designed to help you understand your role.
     a. Concentrate on God's plan for YOU.
     b. Trust that God will take care of changing your spouse.

  4. Responsibility.
     a. God has placed within each person certain abilities.
     b. Responding to those abilities is called "responsibility."
     c. Attempting to respond in areas that are not our assignment is taking on the responsibility of the other spouse.
     d. If you have done that, repent and trust God to change your spouse.

C. Leaving and cleaving [Genesis 2:24].

  1. It is Based on Covenant Relationship.
     a. This does not mean severing relationships with parents.
        1) Jesus left His Father to establish covenant with Church.
        2) He maintained relationship with His Father.
     b. It means establishing a primary relationship with your spouse.

  2. Jesus to Church.
     a. Jesus covenanted with her.
        1) Loved, cared for, nurtured, and gave His life for her.
        2) Gave up all that being God meant to establish relationship with her [Philippians 2:6,7].
     b. As commitment is with Jesus and the Church, so it is with husband and wife.

  3. Church to Jesus—Gives up all to follow Jesus [Luke 14:33].

Personal Application

Week 3

Special Scriptures

ROLES

    4. Husband and wife.
       a. Marital relationship must be priority over all other earthly relationships.
       b. Don't sacrifice your primary relationship for a secondary one.

D. Roles of Jesus and the Church.

    1. Jesus to Church. *(HNWK)*
       a. Reassures her of His love and loyalty [Matthew 28:20b].
       b. Provides her all the Kingdom of God offers [Luke 12:32].
       c. Forgives her [Luke 23:34].
       d. Heals her [Mark 1:29-34].
       e. Serves her [John 13:1-7; Mark 10:45].
       f. Leads her [Luke 9:23].
       g. Gives Godly purpose to lives [Luke 5:8-10].
       h. Intercedes for her [Hebrews 7:25].
       i. Comforts her [Philippians 2:1-2].
       j. Exhorts and encourages her [Romans 15:5 NIV].
       k. Gives her strength [Ephesians 3:16].
       l. Example of God's heart [John 14:9].
       m. Teaches her [Luke 4:31,32; Matthew 7:28,29].
       n. Respects authority [Luke 20:22-25].
       o. Opposes sin [Luke 19:45].
       p. Discerns spirits [Matthew 16:23].
       q. Has authority over spiritual darkness [Luke 4:36].

    2. Church to Jesus, or to Others by His Example and Direction.
       a. Loves Him [Matthew 22:37].
       b. Honors Him [1 Timothy 1:17].
       c. Esteems, respects, and reverences Him [Revelation 4:11].
       d. Caretaker of what He has provided [Hebrews 12:28].
       e. Heals in His Name [Mark 16:18].
       f. Forgives as Has Been Forgiven [Matthew 6:14; 2 Corinthians 5:18].
       g. Exhorts by His Example [Hebrews 3:13].
       h. Comforts as Has Been Comforted [2 Corinthians 1:4].
       i. Does His will as the Spirit leads [Romans 8:14].
       j. Serves [John 13:13-16].
       k. Respects God-given authority [Romans 13:1-2].
       l. Intercedes [1 Thessalonians 5:17; Ephesians 6:18].
       m. Takes authority over spiritual darkness by the Power of His name [1 John 4:1; Mark 16:17].
       n. Ministers [Matthew 28:18-20].
       o. Nurtures [1 Corinthians 12:25].

E. Roles of Husband and Wife.

    1. **HUSBAND – Reassuring Covering** [Ephesians 5:25; 1 Peter 3:7].
       a. Be sensitive to your wife's needs; spirit, soul, and body.
       b. **Comfort** her as Holy Spirit directs, not as you feel.
       c. Minister to her from the Word.
       d. Respond with empathy, not sympathy.
       e. Do not abdicate your protection of her or cause her to feel abandoned.

Week 3

Personal Application

Special Scriptures

ROLES

2. **WIFE - Helper** [Genesis 2:18; Proverbs 31:10-12].
   a. Comes from Hebrew word "to surround."
   b. This is not a secondary but a vital role.
   c. Surround your husband with:
      1) **Support**.
      2) **Exhortation**.
      3) **Comfort**.
   d. Make available to him all the godly qualities within you to help him develop into the man he is called to be.

3. **HUSBAND - Leader** [1 Corinthians 11:3].
   a. Final **leadership** responsibility lies with husband.
   b. Exercise in love the authority given to you.
      1) Will bring stability to family.
      2) Be an example of standing firm despite circumstances.
   c. Resist the enemy, not your family.
   d. Receive godly counsel and wisdom from your wife.

4. **WIFE - Supporter** [Ephesians 5:22-24; 1 Peter 3:1,2].
   a. Husbands need to be **respected** and **honored**.
      1) Even if they are not acting like it.
      2) Honor the authority of God and He will change the man.
   b. God has given men the desire to conquer.
   c. When a wife is supportive, her husband is more willing to take the initiative.
   d. Criticism can hinder him from going forth boldly.
   e. **Respect the authority God has placed in him.**
      1) Work together in decision-making.
      2) Don't side with children against him.

5. **HUSBAND - Provider** [1 Timothy 5:8; Deuteronomy 6:6-9].
   a. **Provide** your family with not only physical needs but also **all that kingdom living includes**.
   b. Be the primary source of Gospel teaching for your family. *(needs work)*
   c. Be instrumental in bringing each family member into salvation and the fullness of the Spirit.
   d. Give godly purpose to lives.

6. **WIFE - Administrator** [Proverbs 31:13-27].
   a. Skillful and godly **administration** will increase and multiply that which your husband provides.
   b. As the Spirit leads, wisely invest that which is saved to produce even more.
   c. To know God's plan, must spend time daily in Word and prayer with Him.
   d. Prosperity comes from seeking the face of the Lord and knowing Him.

Week 3

Personal Application

Special Scriptures

ROLES

7. **HUSBAND - Example of God's Heart** [Mark 10:44; Matthew 6:14,15; Mark 6:17,18].
    a. God's heart is always for **reconciliation** and **restoration**.
    b. This includes **forgiving**, **serving**, and **healing**.
        1) Be quick and constant in forgiveness.
            a) Does not depend on repentance of others.
            b) Jesus forgave before He was asked.
        2) Serve your wife and family with a humble spirit and a joyful heart.
        3) Step out boldly to be an instrument of God's healing to your family.

– Lead from the front

8. **WIFE - Reflection of God's Love** [1 John 4:19-21; John 13:35].
    a. Caring for your husband and family should be a joy and reflect heart of a **servant**.
    b. **Forgive** quickly, not keeping a record of wrongs.
    c. Draw strength from the Word.
        1) Gives you the ability to weather circumstances.
        2) Helps you minister **healing** and wholeness.
    ✱d. Words carry the power of life or death [Proverbs 18:21].
        1) Use words to nurture.
        2) Never destroy with them.

9. **HUSBAND - Lover, Champion** [Ephesians 5:25-28; 1 Corinthians 7:3-5; Ruth 3:9].
    a. Wives need to be **loved** and cherished.
    b. They are sensitive to motives.
    c. You must **reassure** your wife of your love for her.
    d. Reinforce your **faithfulness** with actions.
    e. **Honor** her with your appearance.
    f. Be a gentle, faithful lover ministering to her needs.

10. **WIFE - Lover, Companion** [1 Corinthians 7:3-5; Song of Solomon 2:16; 1 Peter 3:4-6].
    a. Your first **ministry** is to your husband.
        1) Do not neglect him.
        2) Make sure you have God's desire for other ministry.
    b. Remain well-kept and pleasing in appearance as an honor to him.
    c. Submit your flesh and emotions to the control of the Holy Spirit.
    d. Honor and **respect** him; compliment him.
    e. Be the physical **lover** he needs.

Week 3

Personal Application

Special Scriptures

ROLES

11. **HUSBAND - Example of God's Sovereignty** [Hebrews 3:13; 2 Corinthians 10:5,6].
    a. Take firm, uncompromising **stand against sin**.
       1) Hate the sin.
       2) Love the sinner.
    b. Keep family on track with Lord; point out areas needing correction.
    c. Mix **exhortation** with love and **encouragement**.
    d. Always edify with words even when challenging to excellence.
    e. **Respect God-given authority** for your authority to be respected.

12. **WIFE - Reflection of God's Creativity** [1 Corinthians 12:7; Titus 2:3-5].
    a. Each woman has unique talents and **gifts**.
    b. Don't compare yourself with others but allow God to develop what is uniquely you.
    c. You reflect a specific aspect of God's personality and **ministry** flowing from you will reflect that to others.
    d. Your gifts and talents should complement those of your husband and, likewise, his gifts should complement yours.
    e. Couple should flow in harmony even if you are ministering or working separately.

13. **HUSBAND - Intercessor, Warrior** [James 4:7; James 5:16].
    a. You are chief **intercessor** for your wife and family.
    b. You are responsible for **spiritual warfare** on behalf of your wife and family.
    c. **Take authority over the spirits of darkness** that come against your family.
    d. Be Spirit-led in **discernment** of enemy activity and fleshly motives in your family.

14. **WIFE - Intercessor, Discerner** [Ephesians 6:18; 1 Thessalonians 5:17].
    a. Your **intercession** for your husband and family brings you assurance of God's hand in their lives.
    b. Exercise **authority over the enemy** in the name of Jesus.
    c. You are your husband's chief intercessor.
    d. Do not fear the work of the enemy; be alert to his attacks.
    e. Ask the Holy Spirit to develop **discernment** within you and to clothe you with wisdom.

Week 3

Personal Application

Special Scriptures

ROLES

SUGGESTIONS:

1. **Men** read your favorite Gospel in light of what Jesus was to the Church and did for the Church. Compare this to your relationship with your wife.

2. **Women** read your favorite Gospel in light of how the Church responded to Jesus. Compare this to your relationship with your husband.

3. **Both husband and wife** - keep in mind that this lesson discusses YOUR responsibility to God, not your spouse's responsibility to you. Do not criticize your spouse. Remain in faith regarding what the Word says about him or her. Agree with God and His Word, not with what Satan says.

4. This is not a lesson about headship and submission. It is a lesson about dual responsibility in marriage. Perhaps, though, it has changed the way you previously viewed the roles of husband and wife.

5. If you are far from fulfilling your role, trust in the Lord to bring you into the fullness of it. Don't receive condemnation. Remember, God is not finished with any of us yet.

WEEK 3

PERSONAL APPLICATION

SPECIAL SCRIPTURES

SOWING AND REAPING

A. Spiritual Law.

1. *"Be not deceived: God cannot be mocked. A man reaps what he sows. The one who sows to please his sinful nature, from that nature will reap destruction; the one who sows to please the Spirit, from the Spirit will reap eternal life. Let us not become weary in doing good, for at the proper time we will reap a harvest if we do not give up"* [Galatians 6:7-9 NIV].
    a. Like a natural law, it is destined by God to fulfill the purpose for which it was created.
    b. Ignorance does not stop it from operating.
        1) If someone is ignorant of the law of gravity and jumps from a window, they will still hit the ground.
        2) This would truly be a case of perishing for the lack of knowledge [Hosea 4:6].
    c. We are guaranteed a harvest [Galatians 6:7-9].
    d. We will reap a harvest resulting from what we have sown.

2. Seed Sowing.
    a. Seed selection is either from God or from Satan.
        1) *"This day I call heaven and earth as witnesses against you that I have set before you life and death, blessings and curses. Now choose life, so that you and your children may live"* [Deuteronomy 30:19,20 NIV].
        2) Jesus (Life) always sows life/enemy who sows death. [John 10:10].
    b. No seed is neutral.
    c. We are always sowing; consequently, we are always reaping.
    d. When we are born again, we are directed to choose only life-giving seeds [Romans 8:5,6].
    e. Old habits cause us to choose seed from the wrong bag.

3. Types of Seed We Sow.
    a. Words.
        1) "Our children are so rebellious," or *"All our children are taught of the Lord and great is the peace of our children."*
        2) "I just can't do anything right," or *"I can do all things through Christ Who strengthens me."*
        3) "We've never had anything and we're never going to have anything," or *"You still the hunger of those you cherish; their sons have plenty, and they store up wealth for their children."*
    b. Attitudes.
        1) Humility vs. pride; gratitude vs. bitterness; selfishness vs. agape love.
        2) Joy vs. sorrow; eagerness vs. reluctance; acceptance vs. judgment.
    c. Actions.
        1) Acceptance vs. rejection; freely giving with a willing heart vs. demanding others to reach out first.
        2) Kindness vs. violence; unconditional love vs. keeping track of wrongs; praise vs. criticism.

PERSONAL APPLICATION

SPECIAL SCRIPTURES

Bad
Have to
Sarcasm

Good
Please
I need you to

In all situations you can speak of good seed. Our children are taught of the Lord and great is the peace of our children.

SOWING AND REAPING

4. How We Sow.
   a. We are always sowing into lives—our own, our spouse's, our children's, others.
   b. The heart is the soil [Jeremiah 4:3,4].
   c. Types of soil (hearts)[Matthew 13:18-23].
      1) Rocky or thorny soil (hard heart) makes it difficult to produce a crop.
      2) Soil should be well watered by the Word of God.
         a) Crops grow better.
         b) Weeding is easier.
   d. Soil needs to be prepared to receive the seed [Jeremiah 4:3].
      1) In ourselves this is done by prayer and the Word.
      2) For others, we help prepare their hearts through intercessory prayer and spiritual warfare.

B. Factors of the Harvest.
   1. Time Factor.
      a. Harvesting occurs in a different season than the sowing.
      b. After preparing the soil and planting the seed, water the seed with the Word.
      c. Fertilize the crop with your actions [James 2:26].
      d. Don't dig up your seed to see how it is doing.
      e. Don't harvest an immature crop [Mark 4:26-29].
         1) Crop will first appear as blade, not mature plant.
         2) Don't lose hope when it does not appear as what you have sown.
         3) Give it time to mature.
   2. Multiplication Factor.
      a. We always reap in kind what sown. *"For whatever a man sows that, and that only is what he will reap"* [Galatians 6:7 Amplified].
      b. We always reap more than sown [Hosea 8:7; Matthew 13:8].
      c. Each new multiplication of crop provides seed for future sowing.
      d. How downward spirals are created in marriage.
         1) They begin as a single seed that Satan gives us to plant. (Usually the seed is a thought.)
         2) We accept the seed, plant it, and reap the harvest.
         3) Further seed is then provided for more sowing and a larger crop is the result.
         4) Small areas of irritation can become major areas of contention.

WEEK 4

PERSONAL APPLICATION

Make a list of 5 times ea day you spoke wrong & how do right next time. and 5 times you spoke good.

Break soil w/ word of God

Place the word all over your home. Tapes, plaques, books, stickers, stamps

SPECIAL SCRIPTURES

SOWING AND REAPING

C. Recognizing Crops.

1. In ourselves, our spouse, our children, others.

2. Good Crops.
    a. Discover what seeds have been sown to harvest good crops.
    b. Carefully select more seed of the same type to continue good crops.

3. Undesirable Crops.
    a. Repent. *(Turn Away from)*
    b. This is like a weed killer and crops begin to die immediately.
        1) Crops may take time to fully die.
        2) There may even appear to be a growth spurt.
        3) Don't get discouraged.
    c. Do not receive condemnation from the enemy.
    d. Allow God to restore in areas of undesirable crops as you sow good ones [Joel 2:25].
    e. Repent immediately anytime you catch yourself sowing the wrong seeds [1 John 1:9; Deuteronomy 22:9].

D. Sowing Good Crops.

1. Choose seed from God's bag [Deuteronomy 30:19].
    a. Choose the Word to speak and godly characteristics to sow.
    b. Ask God to give you seed for sowing [2 Corinthians 9:10].

2. Prepare the Soil [Jeremiah 4:3].
    a. For yourself—spend time in prayer and the Word.
    b. For others—spend time in intercession and spiritual warfare.

3. You must speak forth the Word to sow it.
    a. Even God speaks His Word to bring it forth.
    b. Genesis 1:3,6,9,11; Isaiah 55:11.

4. Fertilize seed with actions appropriate to harvest you are believing to receive [James 2:26].

5. Realize that the enemy seeks to plant his seeds in your thoughts.
    a. Guard your thoughts [2 Corinthians 10:5].
    b. Think on those things given by the Lord [Philippians 4:8].

E. Avoiding Strife. *(do not envy others)*

1. *"For where envying and strife is, there is confusion and every evil work"* [James 3:16 KJV].

2. *"It is an honor for a man to cease from strife and keep aloof from it"* [Proverbs 20:3a Amplified].

3. It takes two to perpetuate strife. If one does not respond, there can be no strife. *(one of us must stop it)*
    a. One spouse must take an active stand against strife.
    b. This is not a passive ignoring or a defiant silence.

WEEK 4

PERSONAL APPLICATION

SPECIAL SCRIPTURES

Pray - outgrow root system & die

Teach children good/bad seed

Their actions are your harvest

Don't judge - deal with.

— TV —

SOWING AND REAPING

    c.   Strife is very much like a merry-go-round. Is easier to stop when it first begins spinning than when is going full bore [Proverbs 15:1].

4. Is more important to avoid strife than to appear justified [Matthew 23:12].
    a. Your spouse is not the enemy, Satan is [Ephesians 6:12].
    b. Sow love when the other sows strife [Romans 12:21; Philippians 2:3; Galatians 5:14,15].
    c. When you sow peace and harmony, you are guaranteed a harvest of like kind in greater measure [Galatians 6:7-9].
    d. There can be no strife if the second person refuses to yield to it.

5. Only the Power of God Can Change a Pattern of Strife in a Relationship.
    a. Sheer will power and determination are not enough.
    b. An excellent method of yielding to God is a "strife break."

6. Strife Break.
    a. Give each other permission to call a strife break anytime. [+ honor]
    b. Calling a strife break is admitting that both of you, including yourself, are in strife. (Do not say, "You're causing strife.")
    c. Simply say, "Strife Break."
    d. Yield your most unruly member (your tongue) to the Spirit [James 3:3-10].
    e. If you are baptized in the Holy Spirit, we recommend you pray together in the Spirit for three minutes - no more, no less.
        1) If longer, you will be reluctant to do it.
        2) If shorter, it will not be effective in breaking the strife.
    f. If you are not familiar with praying in the Spirit, we will be learning about it in Lesson 7. If strife is a problem in your relationship and you want to know more about this now, check with your leaders.
    g. By praying in the Spirit, you will be sowing to the Spirit and not to the flesh [Galatians 6:8].
    h. Your harvest will come from what you have sown.

WEEK 4

PERSONAL APPLICATION

Jusify right + cause strife = wrong
Flesh not Lord
↓
Whiny
pain

Prayer language

SPECIAL SCRIPTURES

FORGIVENESS

A. Forgiveness should be at the very heart of our Christian walk.

   1. We have no problem with the concept; It is easy to talk about.

   2. It is harder to do.
      a. We harbor "justified" unforgiveness.
      b. We look for signs of "true" repentance.
      c. We remind others of their need to repent before we will forgive.

   3. We are often self-righteous and quick to find fault.

B. Definition of Forgiveness.

   1. To grant free pardon for or remission of any offense or debt; to give up all claim.

   2. God grants pardon freely.
      a. Jesus paid the price.
      b. We, also, are to grant pardon freely, not extract payment for forgiveness.

C. Forgiveness is a Command of God.

   1. As we forgive, we are forgiven [Matthew 6:14,15 Amplified]. *same size bucket*
      a. God sets the standard.
      b. God can only forgive us in measure we are willing to forgive others.

   2. Unforgiveness holds us in bondage [Matthew 18:23-35].
      a. We seek to be forgiven but hold on to the offenses of those who have offended us.
      b. If we do not forgive, we are *"delivered ...to the tormentors"* [Matthew 18:34].
         1) Unforgiveness can manifest in physical and mental illness.
         2) Unforgiveness is often the root of demonic strongholds.
         3) Unforgiveness affects the one refusing to forgive as well as the one not forgiven.

   3. Unforgiveness blocks the promises of God [Matthew 5:23,24; Mark 11:25].
      a. God instructs us to forgive our brother **before** we pray.
      b. In order for us to operate in faith, our hearts must be right toward others.
      c. The Word covers both those we have offended [Matthew 5:23,24] and those who have offended us [Mark 11:25].
         ✱1) If we have offended—we are to initiate forgiveness.
         ✱2) If we have been offended—we are to initiate forgiveness.
         3) We usually judge others by their actions but ourselves by our intentions.
         4) We want judgment for others but mercy for ourselves.
      d. Our justification only perpetuates the sin and continues the void between us and the one who has offended us.
      e. It is important not to speak to others regarding the offense [Proverbs 17:9].
         1) Not referring to a counseling situation in which help is being sought.
         2) This is referring to times of sharing an offense just to gain sympathy and defense.

PERSONAL APPLICATION

SPECIAL SCRIPTURES

I will forgive you when you show it.

in your mind - torments

unforgiveness is like acid - it eats at you.

Forgive
Thanks
Request

sup. close friends

FORGIVENESS

4. The repentance of our spouse (or anyone else) is not necessary for forgiveness.
    a. The act of forgiveness releases the offender to repentance [Romans 2:4].
    b. Both Jesus [Luke 23:34] and Stephen [Acts 7:60] sought forgiveness for their offenders while they were dying, even though there was no repentance on the part of those who sought their death.

5. There is no limit to the number of times we are to forgive [Matthew 18:22].
    a. Love keeps no record of wrongs [1 Corinthians 13:5].
    b. Love covers a multitude of sin [1 Peter 4:8].
    c. If your spouse is committing repetitive sin,
        1) Forgive as God does [Isaiah 43:25; Psalm 103:12].
        2) God does not remember a forgiven sin.
            a) When we forgive, we should not bring up past sin.
            b) Forgetting means not actively remembering.
            c) Treat each new offense as if it had never happened before.
            d) Never bring up past offenses that have been forgiven.
        3) This is not possible in our own human power.
            a) It is only possible through the power of God.
            b) His nature dwelling within us enables us to forgive and trust again.

6. Forgiveness is an act of the will, not a feeling. *Act of Obedience*
    a. You must will (decide) to forgive and your feelings will follow.
    b. Put your will in agreement with God's will and be led of the Spirit [Psalm 103:2-4].
    c. Ask God to show you how He sees the offender.
        1) Only through His heart of love and compassion are we able to forgive those who have wounded us.
        2) Our own feelings of pain and anger are overridden by His great love for them.

D. We need to examine ourselves, not our spouse [Matthew 7:1-5; Luke 6:37].

1. Forgiving spouse.
    a. When you have forgiven much, you can expect to receive much love [Luke 7:47].
    b. God does not categorize sin as "big" and "little." We cannot justify our "little" sin of self righteousness because of our spouse's "big" sin.
    c. To God, sin is sin [1 John 2:4; 1 John 3:4].
    d. When we walk in judgment we often become just like the one we judge.
    e. We must give up all claim, totally release the offender in order to walk in total freedom.

2. Through the power of God there is no obstacle to forgiveness.
    a. "I can't forgive" really means "I won't forgive."
    b. Unforgiveness in our heart hinders our walk with God.
        1) Our own forgiveness is blocked [Matthew 6:14,15].
        2) We will not prosper with sin in lives [Proverbs 28:13].
    c. Often we tend to blame the one we refuse to forgive when we experience the negative effects of unforgiveness.

Personal Application

"Your messing up" - Hardens Heart

Special Scriptures

FORGIVENESS

3. Bitterness [Hebrews 12:15].
   a. Bitterness is the result of long-term unforgiveness.
   b. The ultimate effect of bitterness is that many are defiled.
   c. If we allow bitterness to take root, it will:
      1) Destroy us.
      2) Affect other people.
      3) Give birth to other sin.
      4) Harden our heart and cause it to grow cold.
      5) Crush love and often destroy it.

4. Taking Up the Offense of Another.
   a. It is easy to take up the offense of our spouse or children when they have been offended.
   b. Proverbs 26:17 - Just like with the dog, once you have picked up the offense, how do you let it go?
      1) Repent of having taken up another's offense.
      2) Help the one offended to forgive.
      3) You must forgive the offender even if the one offended will not.
   c. When your spouse is offended, help him/her to forgive.
      1) Respond with empathy, not sympathy.
         a) Empathy = understanding that they have been wounded and helping them to forgive.
         b) Sympathy = just feeling sorry for them.
      2) Don't feel sorry for them, but help them get healed.

E. Reconciliation.

1. Forgiving Ourselves.
   a. Often before we can forgive others, we need to forgive ourselves.
      1) Jesus has forgiven us.
      2) If we don't forgive ourselves, we hold ourselves in a higher position than the Lord. This is pride.
   b. We cannot love and forgive others if we don't love ourselves [Matthew 22:39].

2. We cannot afford even small areas of unforgiveness in our marriage.
   a. Jesus put hostility to death [Ephesians 2:14-16].
   b. He has destroyed the dividing wall between us.
   c. Don't allow the enemy to rebuild the wall of unforgiveness.

3. How to Forgive.
   a. Recognize it is an act of the will, not a feeling.
      1) Ask God to show you how He sees the offender.
      2) Allow His compassion to well up within you.
      3) Choose to forgive; be obedient.
      4) Take to the cross the hurt you received and exchange it for the love and mercy of Jesus.
   b. Confess it as done.
   c. Remember the forgiven offense no more. (Don't dwell on it.)

Personal Application

Special Scriptures

← With the kids

Not forgiving yourself — placing yourself above God. WRONG
↗
James + I 💡

No Grace for anyone

FORGIVENESS

    d.   Sow good seed and speak God's Word instead of the problem.
    e.   Bless the one you have forgiven [Matthew 5:44].

WORD FROM THE LORD

(Given to Mike and Marilyn Phillipps when they were writing this manual)

As we have been preparing this, God has spoken to us that there are some who feel there is nothing to forgive, nothing between the two. He has told us that you will recognize the word "disappointment." There has been much disappointment between the two of you and you need to forgive and set each other free in this area. This applies also to areas in which children have disappointed you.

For others He has said the hurt is so deep and so enormous that it is going to be a slow, step-by-step healing. Be encouraged. He goes before you and makes the path straight. The healing is coming. Do not be overwhelmed or dismayed. You cannot begin to imagine the joyful love that awaits you two. It has been preserved in the Father's heart all these years just for the appointed time. Soon you will begin to glimpse its beginning.

And then there are some who cannot yet look beneath the surface. On the surface all is calm and you fear that if you look any deeper, things may not be all you want them to be. The Lord would have you know that there is more—much more, but you must take the step of faith and trust that the glory to come will surpass the present beauty.

Week 5

Personal Application

Special Scriptures

FAITH VISION AND TRUST

A. Faith.

1. In order for our marriages to conform to God's blueprint, we must begin to see things as God sees them.
   a. Often we are far from what God says we should be.
   b. Faith carries us through as God completes the changes.

2. Definition of Faith.
   a. Strong's Concordance: "assured, convinced, persuaded, or trust (in God)."
   b. *"Faith is the substance of things hoped for, the evidence of things not seen"* [Hebrews 11:1 KJV].

3. Two Components of Faith [Romans 10:10 KJV].
   a. Believe in heart.
   b. Confess with mouth. (Faith is voice-activated.)

4. Sequence of Faith in Operation.
   a. We must believe first, then speak.
      1) *"I believed; therefore I have spoken"* [2 Corinthians 4:13 NIV].
      2) *"...but believes that what he says will happen, it will be done for him"* [Mark 11:23 NIV].
   b. There is a difference between faith and merely quoting the Word with no heart belief.
      1) Constant repetition can be based in fear, not faith.
      2) Sometimes those constantly quoting the Word are trying to convince others, not themselves, of God's truth in the situation.

B. Faith Requires Vision.

1. In order to overcome, we must see things as God sees them.
   a. *"Where there is no vision, the people perish"* [Proverbs 29:18 KJV].
   b. We must know what God has promised for life-giving faith to manifest.
   c. Vision gives life.

2. God has a faith vision for each person and situation.
   a. He is waiting for us to line up with His will and agree with His vision.
   b. When we agree with God and His Word, we bring the will of God to pass on earth [Matthew 18:19; Matthew 6:10].

3. The devil desires destruction of each person and situation.
   ※ a. Agreeing with circumstances (what can be seen with the natural eye) is agreeing with enemy (when the circumstances are contrary to God's will).
   b. Doubt and unbelief are faith in Satan's lies.

   he wants you to give up

4. We choose with whom we will agree.

Personal Application

Special Scriptures

2. for each other, self, & children

Children
    Psalm 1 - truth
    2 Corinthians 1:4 +3

FAITH VISION AND TRUST

C. Obtaining the Vision from God.

1. Seek the Lord regarding person or situation and ask Him for His vision.
   a. This is not selfish, manipulative seeking.
   b. This is not, "Lord, make them what I want them to be."

2. When we obtain God's vision, we begin to see the person or situation as God sees them.
   a. *"For my thoughts are not your thoughts, neither are your ways my ways," declares the Lord. "As the heavens are higher than the earth, so are my ways higher than your ways and my thoughts than your thoughts"* [Isaiah 55:8-9].
   b. *"So we fix our eyes not on what is seen, but on what is unseen"* [2 Corinthians 4:18a NIV].

   (handwritten: doubling blessings)

D. If We Lack Faith to Believe God.

1. Quoting the Word renews our minds.
   a. Speak out scriptures which deal with that subject.
      1) For example, healing:
         a) *"He forgives all my sin and heals all my diseases"* [Psalm 103:3 NIV].
         b) *"He himself bore our sins in his body on the tree, so that we might die to sins and live for righteousness; by his wounds you have been healed"* [1 Peter 2:24 NIV].
      2) This is not blind repetition of the Word.
         a) We are quoting the Word to build faith.
         b) This repetition is not yet faith, but is renewing our mind.
         c) *"So then faith comes by hearing, and hearing by the word of God."* [Romans 10:17].
         d) When our mind is renewed to truth, it causes the Word to drop into our heart becoming belief. (This is faith.)
         e) *"…but be transformed by the renewing of your mind…"* [Romans 12:2].
      3) When the scripture becomes real to us, we begin to BELIEVE God wants us healed.
   b. We can then proclaim the Word with belief.

2. Faith must rest in God, not our own ability.
   a. *"…so that your faith might not rest on men's wisdom, but on God's power"* [1 Corinthians 2:5 NIV].
   b. Power of God, not formula, that causes faith to work.

3. Begin confessing what the Lord has shown from His Word as a reality in the natural.
   a. See God's promises through eyes of faith [Hebrews 11:1 NIV].
   b. Faith vision does not mean ignoring circumstances, it means overcoming them [Romans 4:19-21].
   c. Abraham faced his circumstances (his 100 year-old body and Sarah's barren womb) and still believed God for the promise.

WEEK 6

Personal Application

Special Scriptures

Desire to change, sow (God word) in your heart
(repetition)
faith is fruit of the spirit

FAITH VISION AND TRUST

4. God *"...calls those things that are not as though they were"* [Romans 4:17 NIV].
   a. He does not call those things that are as though they were not.
   b. For example, when we are sick,
      1) *"I am not sick"* is calling that which is as though it were not.
      2) *"I am healed"* is calling that which is not as though it were.
   c. Faith does not ignore reality; it believes God's Word is more powerful.

E. What Is Reality?

   1. When God reveals His will, we need to keep our eyes fixed on the reality of His Word, not the natural circumstances [Hebrews 11:1 NKJV].

   2. This may be difficult because we have been trained incorrectly by the world.
      a. We have been taught that what is real must affect our senses and be accomplished in the natural first. He walks in *"...the futility of the mind"* [Ephesians 4:17 Amplified].
      b. We must learn that true reality is seen and accomplished in the spirit before it is manifested in the natural [Romans 4:19-21].
      c. To believe for changes in our spouse, our marriage, or our children we must believe what God says regarding them no matter what the circumstances are saying.

F. The Importance of the Word of God.

   1. God's Word is His will.
      a. It is God's faith vision for us and our lives.
      b. Agreeing with His Word and speaking it forth causes God's will to be accomplished on the earth [Matthew 18:19; 6:10].

   2. The Word of God is the native language of those born-again.
      a. Just as we teach our children to speak, so our Father teaches us His Word.
      b. Just as we become excited when our children learn to talk, so our Father rejoices when we begin to speak His language.
      c. Just as we would be surprised if our children spoke forth a foreign language other than what we had taught them, doubt and unbelief should be a foreign language to us.
      d. Children learn to speak through time spent with parents.
         1) Time spent with our Father will determine how we speak.
         2) We fellowship with our Father through His Word.
            1 Peter 3:12 Amplified: *"...And His ears are attentive to their prayers."*
         3) He wants to hear us speak His Word regarding our spouse and marriage.

   3. Praying the Word which contains God's power.
      a. The Word is neither a religious ritual nor a manipulative formula.
      b. He watches over it [Jeremiah 1:12 NIV].

Week 6

Personal Application

Special Scriptures

Power come from word of God

where did you learn that?

FAITH VISION AND TRUST

        c. It never returns to Him without accomplishing that for which He sent it [Isaiah 55:11 Amplified].
        d. God sends forth His angels to accomplish His Word [Psalm 103:20].
        e. Speaking the Word causes our faith vision to be manifested.
        f. There is power in agreement. When we pray the Word we are in agreement with will of God [Matthew 18:19].

G. Our Responsibility When Believing.

    1. Just as God is responsible to fulfill His Word, we also have responsibility when we stand in faith.
        a. We are to remain in fellowship with the Lord to keep His Word in our hearts.
            1) Fellowship with the Lord [John 15:7 NIV].
            2) Keep your heart in God's Word [Matthew 12:34 KJV].
            3) This is the key to standing in faith.
        b. Spending time with the Lord increases desire to see His will come to pass.
            1) Are you having trouble believing for something regarding your spouse or your marriage?
            2) Spending more time with Jesus will build your faith.

    2. You need to make sure you have no unforgiveness in your heart [Matthew 5:23,24; Mark 11:25].
        a. Remember you are to initiate forgiveness whether you have offended or have been offended.
        b. If you continue to hold unforgiveness, it is difficult to stand in faith.

    3. **Perhaps most important of all, in order to stand in faith, we must be assured that God loves us.**
        a. If this is not the case, we must first settle this issue in our heart.
        b. It is difficult to believe God wants to bless us if we do not know He loves us.
            1) All of His promises are for His children [Jeremiah 29:11; Mark 7:27; Psalm 84:11].
            2) Are you His child? Since you are, His promises are for **you**.
            3) When we see someone else blessed by God, we need to rejoice with them because God wants to bless **all** His children.
        c. His love for us needs to be unshakable in us.
            1) If you are unsure of His love, find scriptures that tell you how much He loves you.
            2) Quote those scriptures to yourself so that your ears can hear of His love for you [Romans 10:17].
            3) Allow His love to become real to you.
        d. Once assured of His love, you can stand, believing His promises are for you.

H. Trust Is the Partner of Faith.

    1. Definition of Trust.
        a. Strong's Concordance: "to convince, to rely (by inward certainty), yield, obey, persuade."
        b. Dictionary: "reliance on the integrity, justice, etc., of a person, or on some quality or attribute of a thing; confidence."

Week 6

Personal Application

Special Scriptures

FAITH VISION AND TRUST

2. Trust in Man.
    a. It is almost impossible to trust people sometimes.
        1) They wound, disappoint, and hurt.
        2) Many times our spouse is the one who has done this more than others.
    b. Most couples begin marriage trusting each other, but trust can be lost as years go by.
        1) Trust can be eroded by disappointments and repeated failures.
        2) Trust can be broken by such things as adultery, abuse, or abandonment.
    c. When trust is gone, there is jealousy, doubt, fear, and constant suspicion.
        1) Strife brings confusion and every evil work [James 3:16 KJV].
        2) Trusting in man will always bring disappointment [Jeremiah 17:5 NIV].

3. There Is Only One Way to Rebuild Trust in a Marriage.
    a. When trust in your spouse is broken or eroded, you must place your trust in God, not your spouse.
    b. Forgive the sin and disappointments that have caused the lack of trust.
    c. Trust God to change the circumstances.
        1) He is bigger than the problem and He is able to change our heart [Jeremiah 32:39; Ezekiel 11:19].
        2) He never fails [1 Corinthians 15:57].
        3) He is working on that which concerns us and He will bring it to completion [Psalm 138:8; Philippians 1:6].
    d. Trusting God for change takes pressure off each other.
        1) Trust in the natural is impossible if our spouse is not trustworthy.
        2) Jesus can rebuild trust in our heart even before our spouse is worthy of trust because we trust God, not ourselves, for the outcome.
    e. Trusting God to work in spouse frees him or her to grow.
        1) Trust is not based on performance.
        2) Each spouse is even free to make mistakes knowing that God is bigger than the problem [1 Corinthians 15:57].

4. Believing God's Vision for Our Spouse.
    a. What God's Word says regarding spouse is more real than the circumstances seen.
    b. Seek from His Word how He sees spouse [Romans 12:2].
    c. Write down God's vision [Habakkuk 2:2,3].
    d. Speak God's Word for spouse [Isaiah 55:11].
    e. Meditate on the Word day and night [Psalm 1:2; Psalm 119:148].
    f. Believe God's Word for spouse [Jeremiah 1:12].
    g. Speaking God's Word changes circumstances [Mark 11:24].
    h. Trust God to bring His Word to pass in our life, the life of our spouse, and our marriage [Romans 10:11].

Week 6

Personal Application

Special Scriptures

PRAYING TOGETHER

A. Emphasis on Together.

1. This is perhaps the most important lesson of all.
   a. All the other lessons are the bricks.
   b. This lesson is the mortar.

2. Many husbands and wives have active separate prayer lives.
   a. We still need individual prayer time each day.
   b. Individual prayer is not sufficient for a couple.

3. The only way two can truly become one as God intends is for both to submit themselves to the guidance and direction of the Holy Spirit by praying together.
   a. It is the most intimate thing a husband and wife can do together.
   b. It is essential to the health of a marriage.
   c. It takes dedication, practice, and consistency.

B. Reasons for Praying Together.

1. Our spouse is an intimate prayer partner [Matthew 18:20].

2. We have power of agreement [Matthew 18:19].
   a. Agreeing with God's will brings it to pass on the earth.
   b. There will be more about agreement in next week's lesson.

3. Power in spiritual warfare increases exponentially [Leviticus 26:8]. 5—100 100—10,000
   a. We have authority in Jesus to tear down strongholds and break satanic holds [2 Corinthians 10:4,5 TLB].
   b. We need to "patrol our hedge" together [Job 1:10]. responsibility
   c. There will be more about spiritual warfare in Lesson 11.

C. Guidelines for Praying Together.

1. It is an intimate time between you, your spouse, and God.
   a. Do not criticize spouse's prayers or discuss scriptural validity.
      1) It may make spouse feel reluctant to pray out loud.
      2) If you are guilty of doing this, you need to repent.
      3) Resolve to seek unity in your prayer time together.
      *4) Allow God to bring about growth in your spouse's prayer life.
   b. Your attention to spouse's prayer concerns will give you a better understanding of his/her relationship with God.
      1) Learn to better understand the heart of your spouse.
      2) It is a special privilege to sit in on that conversation with God. Don't abuse it.

2. Together follow Paul's example for prayer: *"I will pray with the spirit, and I will pray with the understanding also"* [1 Corinthians 14:15 KJV].
   a. There is a time to pray in the spirit (tongues) and a time to pray in our native language (with the understanding).
   b. Praying in our native language together.
      1) It takes more maturity than praying in the spirit together.

PERSONAL APPLICATION

SPECIAL SCRIPTURES

anger, yelling
Calendar - protect time*   homeschooling - hedge

Be open to listening, not just hearing, to your spouse and what God has to say to you. (conviction)

WEEK 7

Praying Together

        2) There can be a tendency to manipulate or correct. ("Oh Lord, help him to stop smoking. You know how that bothers me.")
        3) One spouse may desire to pray on and on while the other may feel that only a few words are necessary.

3. Enter into His presence with praise and worship.
   a. Psalm 100:4; Psalm 22:3.
   b. Need not be formalized; just praise Him from your heart.

4. Praying with the understanding (your native language).
   a. Use Philippians 4:6 as a guide.
      1) Thank God for what He has provided and how He has cared.
      2) Present to Him your needs and desires.
         a) The Word says to present a petition.
         b) It is good to write your requests down and keep track of answers to prayer.
      3) When you are praying together, limit prayers to things which concern you as one-flesh.
         a) Use your personal prayer time to cover individual concerns.
         b) Examples: One has a burden for a specific political official. One has a burden for the starving of Ethiopia.
   b. Pray the Word [1 John 5:14,15].
      1) We know we are praying God's will.
      2) It keeps our own opinions out of the prayer.
      3) The Lord watches over His Word [Jeremiah 1:12 NAS]; it will not return void [Isaiah 55:11].

5. Praying in the Spirit (tongues).
   a. One of the most significant things a husband and wife can do for their marriage.
      1) *"Edify and improve"* one-flesh life [1 Corinthians 14:4 Amplified].
         a) We can experience more rapid spiritual growth (spirit).
         b) It can improve our communication (soul).
         c) It can improve our sexual intimacy (body).
      2) When we are in agreement with God, we, therefore, are in agreement with each other.
   b. We submit our most unruly member, the tongue, to direction of Holy Spirit [James 3:8].
   c. As we submit to Him together, we enable Him to mold us and blend us as He desires [Romans 8:26-29].
   d. There may be resistance to praying together in tongues because it "sounds funny."
      1) Get over the embarrassment and into the fullness of God's plan for you.
      2) Pray in your prayer language frequently so that you become freer in it.

6. As a couple, make appointment daily with Jesus and keep it diligently.
   a. The enemy hates for couples to pray together and will use every trick to keep us from doing it.
   b. Don't just talk about it, think about it, or discuss it - DO IT!

Week 7

Personal Application

Special Scriptures

c. Couples hurting too much to even talk can pray together in the spirit and get their marriage healed.
d. One-flesh growth flows out of the strength of prayer time together.

7. The Baptism or Infilling of the Holy Spirit.
   a. In order to pray in the spirit together, we must receive tongues from the Holy Spirit.
   b. The Word of God is clear regarding God's desire.

A SCRIPTURAL STUDY OF THE BASIS FOR THE BAPTISM OF THE HOLY SPIRIT.

Before His ascension into Heaven, Jesus told His disciples to wait in Jerusalem until they were baptized with the Holy Spirit [Acts 1:4,5]. Those to whom He was speaking had been born again when he came to them after His death and resurrection [John 20:22]. It was obvious from what Jesus was telling them in the first chapter of Acts, though, that there was another, separate experience available to them. In Acts 1:8, Jesus promised them that they would receive power and become His witnesses to the ends of the earth. All of those who gathered to hear Jesus loved Him very much and had chosen to follow Him but they lacked courage and boldness. All of them had deserted Him when He was crucified with the exception of John and the women. Peter had even denied knowing Him. They obviously needed the power that it would take to live out their commitment to Him.

In Acts chapter 2, all of the disciples were gathered in one place. Even Mary, the mother of Jesus was there. The Holy Spirit came upon them and they were filled with the Holy Spirit. The first manifestation of this infilling was that they all began to speak in tongues as the Spirit enabled them [Acts 2:4]. These tongues were understood by people from all nations who were in Jerusalem for the feast of Pentecost. This speaking all together in tongues gave the disciples tremendous unity and power such as had not been seen on the earth since God confused the languages at the tower of Babel [Genesis 11:6-9]. When we speak as one and have one heart and purpose, there is power. Speaking in tongues provided for them (and for us) that unity they had not previously had. It enabled them, and now us, to come together with believers from all over the world, speaking different natural languages but speaking together in the spirit. The second manifestation of the Baptism was the boldness with which the disciples began to proclaim the Gospel. These same people who had previously been so afraid and timid were now drawing large crowds with their preaching.

They were suddenly not concerned with what the crowds thought of them or if they were in danger. They had received the power necessary to live the Christian life.

Be assured that Satan knows the power of this experience. He has done much down through the ages to discredit it. In some churches he has even convinced them to give him the credit for the outward manifestations of the Baptism of the Holy Spirit, tongues in particular. He has gotten many people to overlook the experience and to even scoff at it, much to their loss. Without the Baptism of the Holy Spirit, we are very limited in what we can accomplish. We are not "plugged in" to the vital source of supernatural power that the Holy Spirit offers.

The Baptism or the Infilling of the Holy Spirit was not a one-time experience in the history of the church. Throughout the book of Acts, the same experience with the same manifestations occurred over and over again [Acts 8, Acts 10, Acts 19]. The first-century church moved in the spirit in a way that we often covet. Yet this same measure of power and authority is available to the church today if we would only receive it. If the Body of Christ were united today in the

Week 7

Personal Application

Special Scriptures

Praying Together

Holy Spirit power in which the first-century church moved, we would see victory and glory that we only dream of now. We can, however, begin in our home. In each of our lives this power is available the same way it was available to each disciple on the day of Pentecost. We only need to reach out and take it.

In Luke 11:11-13, Jesus tells us that if we who are earthly know how to give our children good things, how much more then will the Father in Heaven give the Holy Spirit to those who ask Him. We know then that we must ask to receive. James tells us that we have not because we ask not [James 4:2]. The Baptism of the Holy Spirit is available to anyone who has asked Jesus to be their Lord and Savior. We need only ask our Father in Jesus' name to baptize us in the Holy Spirit and He does. We can ask Him all by ourselves or we can ask other Spirit-filled Christians to lay hands on us to impart the Baptism [Acts 8:17; Acts 19:6]. Know that when we ask, we receive. Take that promise and receive all that the Holy Spirit has for you.

Tongues are definitely one of the manifestations of the Baptism of the Holy Spirit. This is our own prayer language, not the Gift of Tongues. The Gift of Tongues, one of the nine gifts of the Holy Spirit, is what Paul was talking about in 1 Corinthians 14:5,13,22,23. Scripture tells us that this gift must function in conjunction with the Gift of Interpretation to supernaturally deliver a word from God to the hearers [1 Corinthians 14:27,28]. The prayer language of tongues is what Paul was talking about in 1 Corinthians 14:4,14,15,18,19. This is your personal prayer language which does not require interpretation [Romans 8:26,27] If you do not understand the difference, please continue to study the scriptures and/or ask your leaders for help.

If tongues do not manifest readily when a person receives the Baptism of the Holy Spirit, we should not make excuses or decide that God does not want us to have that gift. Instead we need to seek the Lord as to what is blocking the manifestation. It may simply be an intellectual argument or just embarrassment. It may, however, be something more serious such as previous involvement in occult activities (e.g. horoscopes, ouija boards, automatic writing, etc.). When tongues do not manifest, we need to ask the Holy Spirit for discernment regarding the blockage. We need, however, to be cautious that we remain in the spirit in our attempts to help the individual and not enter into fleshly activities such as "Repeat after me...," grabbing people's jaws and moving their heads around, and other activities designed to force the manifestation of tongues. Tongues do not have to be forced. If they are being blocked, we need only discern the blockage and remove it. They will then readily flow.

When the Holy Spirit speaks through you in tongues, He will give the words but you need to surrender your tongue to Him. That does not mean that you don't make a sound and that God will supernaturally take over your speech. Very often you will become aware of words that are unfamiliar to you and you will tell yourself that they are nonsense. Take a step of faith and speak them out. Once you have been obedient in surrendering your tongue, the Holy Spirit will begin supplying you with a whole new, beautiful language. Begin using that language to praise God and to tell Him of your love for Him. As you use your language daily you will begin to see it increase. That increase and frequent usage will bring you to Paul's desire *to "pray in the Spirit on all occasions"* [Ephesians 6:18 NIV].

WEEK 7

PERSONAL APPLICATION

SPECIAL SCRIPTURES

Jn 14: 16, 17, 26
Jn 7: 37-38
Luke 11: 11-13
Acts 1:8
Acts 2
Acts 4

Romans 8: 25, 27
1 Corth 14: 2, 4, 14

Lauren?

AGREEMENT

A. God intends for us to walk in agreement in our marriage (*Can two walk together, unless they are agreed?"* Amos 3:3 NKJV).

   1. Couples are often told not to walk together if they are not in agreement.
      a. Separation or divorce are erroneously recommended.
      b. One spouse is wrongly told to "go on in ministry" and leave other behind.

   2. Because it is God's desire for us to walk together, we need to learn how to come into agreement.
      a. He has made us one [Genesis 2:24; Matthew 19:5; Ephesians 5:31].
      b. What He has joined is not to be separated [Malachi 2:16; Matthew 19:6].

B. Various Ways Couples Reach Agreement.

   1. Lack of Strife.
      a. They reach a decision without arguing.
      b. They consider the alternatives and pick the best one.

   2. Expert Opinion.
      a. The spouse with most experience or knowledge gives expert advice.
      b. The couple agrees to go with the expert's decision.

   3. Compromise.
      a. Each spouse presents his or her own opinion or desire.
      b. They reach a compromise answer halfway between the two extremes.

   4. Survival of the Fittest.
      a. Both spouses are convinced their opinion is the correct answer.
      b. They battle the decision out until one weakens.
      c. Whichever one lasts the longest wins.

   5. Manipulation.
      a. "If you do it my way, I'll give you ..." (money, sex, a night on the town, etc.).
      b. One spouse forces the other to agree by offering or refusing certain favors.

   6. Logic vs. Emotion.
      a. One spouse is better at logical argument while the other spouse better at an emotional one.
      b. The decision goes in favor of the one who performs best.

   7. Default.
      a. One spouse feels strongly about the subject/other spouse doesn't care.
      b. The decision is made by the one who feels strongest/other one just passes.

   8. Open Door/Closed Door.
      a. This is a favorite among Christians.
      b. If the "door is open," the decision is "yes."
      c. If the "door is closed," the decision is "no."

   9. None of these are agreement God's way [James 4:2,3].

Personal Application

Special Scriptures

AGREEMENT

    10. Without agreement as husband and wife, there is lack of peace [James 3:16].
        a. This opens the door to enemy attack.
        b. It often keeps us out of God's will.
        c. It leads to blaming each other for failures.
           1) "I told you so."
           2) "You always think you're right."

C. Agreement God's Way.

    1. *"Again I tell you, if two of you on earth agree [harmonize together, together make a symphony] about anything and everything, whatever they shall ask, it will come to pass and be done for them by My Father in heaven"* [Matthew 18:19 Amplified].
        a. We are to blend together in agreement like a symphony.
           1) Harmonize means to simultaneously combine tones.
           2) This is blending together as we are, not becoming the same as each other.
        b. God will do the blending if we allow Him the freedom.

    2. Follow Christ's Example.
        a. Jesus always sought to fulfill the will of His Father.
           1) *"...I do not seek My own will but the will of the Father who sent Me"* [John 5:30 NKJV].
           2) *"My food is to do the will of Him who sent Me, and to finish His work"* [John 4:34].
        b. Our agreement must also be based on fulfilling the will of our Father.
           1) The Father has a will for everything we do.
           2) We are not to seek to fulfill our own will.
        c. Agreement based on the will of our Father, assures we will see the answer come to pass.
           1) 1 John 5:14,15 NIV.
           2) Matthew 18:19 [Amplified].

D. How To Know The Will of God.

    1. The Word.
        a. We do not have to ask if it is expressly written in the Word.
           1) Word tells us we are to evangelize, we do not have to ask [Mark 16:15; Matthew 28:19; Acts 1:8].
           2) Word tells us we are to rear our children in a godly manner, we do not have to ask [Deuteronomy 11:19; Isaiah 54:13; Titus 1:6].
           3) Word tells us we are to belong to a local body of believers, we do not have to ask [Hebrews 10:25; Acts 2:42,46].

Week 8

Personal Application

Special Scriptures

Agreement

        b. God's will for us is expressed in His Word to us.
        c. We need to know His Word to know His will.
        d. Word often does not say how, when, where.

    2. Specifics regarding God's will, however, cannot always be found in a chapter and verse of the Bible, such as:
        a. Where and how should we evangelize.
        b. How should we handle a specific situation with one of our children.
        c. What church should we join.
        d. Any other matter for which we cannot find specific guidance in scripture.

E. Seeking God's Will When It Cannot be Found Specifically in the Word.

    1. Ask together *"...whatever **they** shall ask..."* [Matthew 18:19].
        a. It is not enough for one to hear from God and the other go along with it [Deuteronomy 19:15b].
        b. We can have confidence that God will answer [Isaiah 30:21, John 10.3].
        c. God desires each spouse know Him and hear Him [John 10:14].
        d. For agreement, **both** spouses must hear from God [Amos 3:3].

    2. Pray together in the spirit to seek God's will.
        a. When we pray in the spirit (tongues), we are praying the perfect will of God [Romans 8:27].
        b. When we pray in the spirit (tongues), our minds are unfruitful [1 Corinthians 14:14].
            1) We want to keep our own opinions out of our prayer [Proverbs 3:5,6].
            2) We want the will of God, not our will [Isaiah 55:9].

    3. Share with each other what God has said to you.
        a. When God is speaking, both spouses will receive the same answer.
            1) God is not a God of confusion [1 Corinthians 14:33].
            2) God does not want us to be double-minded [James 1:8].
        b. If the answers not the same, one or both is not hearing correctly.
            1) One of you may have God's answer, or
            2) God may have an entirely different answer than either one of you have.
            3) Very often at first we hear our own desires in the matter.

    4. If answers differ, return to praying in the spirit and seeking God's will.
        a. Do not pray that your spouse will "come around" and see things your way.
            1) Our pride often keeps us from admitting we could be wrong.
            2) Past experiences should teach us that we are not always right even when we think we are.
        b. Pray for God's will to be revealed to both of you.

    5. When both spouses have received the same answer, you can be confident that you have heard from God [Luke 11:10].

Week 8

Personal Application

Special Scriptures

AGREEMENT

        a. Agreement reached in this manner is led of the Spirit of God, not our own flesh.
        b. There is peace in the answer when both have received [James 3:17].
        c. One final confirmation—if the decision reached has a consequence directly opposing the Word of God, it is not from God.
            1) Any answer received must line up with the Word of God.
            2) The Spirit and the Word always confirm each other.
            3) More time we spend in the Word of God, the more our minds are transformed to quickly know His will [Romans 12:2].

        d. The time it takes to come into agreement this way is far less than time it takes to unravel a wrong decision.

    6. Husband, in your role of headship, declare that as a couple you will not move without agreement.
        a. This does not deny your role of headship [Ephesians 5:23].
            1) As husband, you are still responsible to God.
            2) This provides added counsel and confirmation.
                a) Proverbs 11:14; Proverbs 15:22 (Amplified).
                b) Even the Word must confirm itself. (Cannot take one isolated scripture.)
        b. Do not allow circumstances imposed on you to pressure or sway you as you seek God's heart.
            1) God knows your time frame and will give answer in His timing.
            2) If a couple is willing to take action without agreement, the enemy will delay the answer.
                a) Deadlines are not deadlines unless God says they are.
                b) The enemy delayed the answer to Daniel for 21 days [Daniel 10].
        c. Refuse second best; always go for true, heartfelt agreement given by the Spirit of God.

F. Bringing God's Will to Pass on the Earth.

    1. *"...it will come to pass and be done for them by my Father in Heaven"* [Matthew 18:19].
        a. Waiting to make sure you have God's will makes it possible to proceed in confidence.
        b. Agreement with the will of God enables His will to come to pass on the earth.

    2. A couple consistently seeking agreement in this manner will begin to focus on the will of God as a way of life.

Week 8

Personal Application

Special Scriptures

FLOWING TOGETHER IN THE SPIRIT

A. Understanding and cooperating with the Holy Spirit as He works in and through us.

1. Often we do not understand the role of the Holy Spirit.
   a. The Holy Spirit is not a thing but a part of the Godhead.
   b. Expect the Holy Spirit to move powerfully in your lives as you pray together and learn to walk in agreement.

2. The work of the Holy Spirit in Jesus' life sets the example of how the Holy Spirit desires to work in our lives.
   a. He was sent to us when Jesus returned to his Father [John 16:7].
   b. He was active in Jesus life.
      1) Jesus was conceived by the Holy Spirit [Matt. 1:18,20; Luke 1:35].
      2) Jesus was filled and anointed by the Holy Spirit [Acts 10:38].
      3) He Prepared Jesus for earthly ministry [Luke 4:1].
         a) Jesus came to earth as a man empowered by the Holy Spirit.
         b) This is how the Holy Spirit desires to work in our lives.
   c. We receive Him when Born-again [John 20:21].
   d. We are baptized in power by Him [Acts 1:8].
   e. We are sealed with Him/He guarantees our inheritance [Ephesians 1:13-14].
   f. He indwells us [I Corinthians 6:19, II Timothy 1:14].
   g. He teaches, regenerates, and renews us [John 14:26, Titus 3:5].

B. Two vital aspects of the Holy Spirit to be balanced in our lives.

1. The inner work is the Fruit of the Spirit.
   a. If we don't exhibit the fruit of the Spirit, our gifts are truly as *"sounding brass" or a "clanging symbol"* [I Corinthians 13:1].
   b. The Fruit is character development.
   c. This work is primarily for our own benefit, but it blesses others.

2. The outer work is the Gifts of the Spirit.
   a. We should not be ignorant of spiritual gifts [I Corinthians 12:1].
   b. Primarily for other's benefit, but blesses us.

C. Fruit of the Spirit *"But the fruit of the Spirit is **love, joy, peace, patience, kindness, goodness, faithfulness, gentleness** and **self-control**"* [Galatians 5:22-23 NIV].

1. It is *"Fruit"* not "fruits".
   a. This is a singular work of the Holy Spirit.
   b. It produces character qualities and spiritual maturity.

2. Qualities of the fruit of the Holy Spirit:
   a. Love-God's unconditional love [I John 3:16].
   b. Joy-Deeper than happiness [John 15:11].
   c. Peace-Security, safety, and tranquility [John 14:27].
   d. Patience-Endurance and steadfastness [James 1:4].
   e. Kindness-Gentleness and integrity [2 Samuel 22:36].
   f. Goodness-Uprightness of heart and life [Romans 15:14].
   g. Faithfulness-Covenant keeping [Psalm 119:90].
   h. Gentleness-Strength under Godly control [Psalm 18:35].
   i. Self Control-Mastery of desires and passions [Proverbs 25:28].

Personal Application

Special Scriptures

FLOWING TOGETHER IN THE SPIRIT

3. The Fruit of the Holy Spirit is for relationships, both with God and each other.
   a. Jesus never miraculously healed relationships.
   b. Jesus never mediated problems in relationships.
   c. Jesus challenged heart problems to heal relational problems.
      4) The mother of James and John, sons of Zebedee [Matthew 20:22-23 and Matthew 20:26-27].
      5) Peter and John [John 21:22].

4. Marriage problems are directly related to issues in our own heart.
   a. We often look elsewhere for improving our marital relationships.
   b. The Lord wants us to look at our own heart, not our spouse's heart.
      1) We need to yield ourselves to the work of the Holy Spirit.
         a) He will bring about the harvest in our one-flesh relationship
         b) There are no short cuts.
      2) Marriage is perhaps the best relationship to test the fruit of the Spirit in our lives.
         a) If fruit is not developed, we may appear to have fruit with casual relationships.
         b) We cannot fake it with our spouse who knows us best.
      3) There is a mistaken view that marriage is supposed to bring out the best in us but the opposite is true.
         a) Marriage is designed to bring the worst to the surface.
         b) Marriage covenant provides security for us as individuals and as a couple during this process of change, healing, and maturity.
      4) Keys to a strong healthy relationship.
         a) Don't look for what is wrong with your spouse but yield to the work of the Holy Spirit within you.
         b) We must not attempt to be the Holy Spirit for our spouse by nagging, control, or manipulation.
         c) We can only be obedient to the Holy Spirit for ourselves.

D. The Holy Spirit produces the fruit:

1. Fruit is the natural result of the indwelling of the Holy Spirit.
   a. It is as natural as apple trees producing apples.
   b. It should not be a struggle.
   c. It begins when He indwells us at salvation.
   d. We will exhibit the fruit of the spirit to the extent that we yield to and are obedient to the Holy Spirit's work within us.

2. Maturity of fruit is the goal.
   a. In the natural-ripened fruit is sweeter and more desirable.
   b. In the spiritual-we desire the same.
   c. Maturity is measured by the degree we have yielded to the work of the Holy Spirit in our lives.

3. A constant battle wars between our flesh and the Holy Spirit.
   a. Jesus was tempted in the three areas that we are [I John 2:16].
   b. He was empowered by the Holy Spirit to resist temptation.
   c. We are empowered by the Holy Spirit to do the same.

Week 9

Personal Application

Special Scriptures

Flowing Together in the Spirit

        e. We do not have to struggle in the natural, with natural laws and regulations, to overcome the pull of our flesh.

        f. The Holy Spirit will transform our hearts and produce the fruit.

    4. Our character weakness are seen best by our spouse.

        a. We need to yield our fleshly actions and desires to the Holy Spirit.

        b. Change does not come by our will power.

        c. This supernatural work of the Holy Spirit brings change.

E. The Gifts of the Spirit

    1. Are an *outflow* of the Holy Spirit through us.

        a. This is in contrast to the Fruit of the Spirit that is a work *within* us.

        b. The Gifts are an indication of God's power, not our ability.

    2. The gifts are given "for the profit of all" [I Corinthians 12:7].

        a. They are the supernatural intervention of God, meeting needs beyond our natural abilities.

        b. They are intended to bless others.

    3. When the Holy Spirit moves through us, we should:

        a. Rejoice in the work of God.

        b. Not be prideful that we were chosen or that He moved mightily through us.

F. There are different Categories of Gifts Mentioned in Scripture

    1. Motive gifts in Romans 12:6-8.

    2. Five-fold ministry gifts in Ephesians 4:11-12.

    3. All the gifts are important and you should be familiar with them.

    4. If you aren't familiar with these ask your pastor for more teaching and/or check your local Christian bookstore for materials.

G. Understanding Each of the Gifts Delineated in Scripture.

    1. The Gifts of the Spirit are found in I Corinthians 12:7-11 NKJV.

        a. "But the manifestation of the Spirit is given to each one for the profit of all: for to one is given the **word of wisdom** through the Spirit,

        b. to another the **word of knowledge** through the same Spirit,

        c. to another **faith** by the same Spirit,

        d. to another **gifts of healing** by the same Spirit,

        e. to another the **working of miracles**,

        f. to another **prophecy,**

        g. to another **discerning of spirits,**

        h. to another **different kinds of tongues,**

        i. to another the **interpretation of tongues.** But one and the same Spirit works all these things, distributing to each one individually as He wills".

Week 9

Personal Application

Special Scriptures

FLOWING TOGETHER IN THE SPIRIT

2. Gifts are given *"to each one"* [I Corinthians 12:7].
   a. Each and every believer receives, not just some.
   b. Many Christians believe gifts are for others, not for themselves.
   c. Many Christians embrace some gifts and not others, depending on their comfort and/or understanding.

3. *"Now concerning spiritual gifts, brethren, I would not have you ignorant"* [1 Corinthians 12:1].
   a. We are commanded to learn about the gifts.
   b. We must not hide behind the excuse that we do not understand or prefer certain gifts.

4. There Are Nine Gifts in Three Categories:
   a. Gifts of Revelation.
      1) Word of Wisdom-revelation of the mind and purpose of God.
      2) Word of Knowledge-revelation or knowledge of a person or thing.
      3) Discerning of Spirits-enables one to see into the spirit realm.
   b. Gifts of Power:
      1) Faith-enables one to sustain an unwavering trust in God.
      2) Gifts of Healing-supernatural power to heal diseases, cast out devils, to make the body whole and healthy.
      3) The Working of Miracles-supernatural power to intervene in the ordinary course of nature.
   c. Gifts of Inspiration.
      1) Prophecy-supernatural utterance in a known tongue.
      2) Different Kinds of Tongues-supernatural utterance in an unknown language.
      3) Interpretation of Tongues-supernatural utterance in the known language of what was spoken in the unknown language.

H. Gifts in Operation.

1. Signs follow believers because of who God is [Mark 16:15-20].
   a. Offspring partake of the same nature, power, attributes and character as their parents.
   b. It should be natural for children of God to move in the supernatural [2 Peter 1:3-4].

2. We need to be available to be used in any gift.
   a. Be sensitive to the leading of the Holy Spirit.
   b. The gifts are given to meet needs of others, not to glorify self.
   c. Rejoice when He chooses to move through you because you were able to help someone, not that you were chosen.

3. The gifts are meant to manifest in our homes.
   a. They are not only for public use.
   b. The home offers a setting in which husband and wife can begin to move in the gifts in a non-threatening atmosphere.
      1) If a mistake is made, we are there to exhort and help each other.
      2) Once we've become comfortable moving in the gifts at home it will be easier in a public setting.

Week 9

Personal Application

Special Scriptures

FLOWING TOGETHER IN THE SPIRIT

    4.   Flowing As One-Flesh In The Gifts.
- a. Become sensitive as to how He would use the two of you together.
- b. When one spouse operates in a gift the other often is a confirmation.
- c. As you spend time in prayer together, expect the Holy Spirit to flow through you as a one-flesh in the gifts.
- d. Sometimes the gifts that manifest first are the gifts of inspiration.
    1) Prophecy, Tongues, and Interpretation of Tongues.
    2) Usually this happens during your prayer time as a couple.
    3) Keep a record of the words that you receive from the Lord.
- e. The gifts are not reserved for "special" people, signs and wonders follow all who believe [Hebrews 2:4].
- f. Teach your children about gifts.
- g. Develop your prayer life and be amazed at the way the Holy Spirit will move through you.

I. The Vision of MMI—Powerhouse Christian Homes.

1. They are to be a light to the lost and oasis of peace to those in turmoil.

2. To be the powerhouse home that God longs for us to be, we must be yielded to the inner working of the Holy Spirit and allow the Holy Spirit to flow through us with His gifts.

3. He wants to use us to change our communities and churches because powerful couples and families help create powerful churches.

4. Search the Word personally to learn what God says about the fruit and gifts of the Spirit.

5. As a one-flesh team we are to walk in the Spirit and not fulfil the lusts of the flesh as well as not be ignorant concerning the spiritual gifts [Galatians 5:16, I Corinthians 12:1]

The role of the Holy Spirit operating in our lives through the Fruit of the Spirit and the Gifts of the Spirit must be balanced for the development of a mature person (and couple) and a mature Body of Christ. The enemy has caused great division in the Body by having individuals, churches, and denominations emphasize one over the other. Jesus, Who is our peace and unity, wants us to be balanced in our understanding of and response to the working of the Holy Spirit in our lives. Then the whole Body of Christ is empowered, as individuals, as couples, and as churches, to be effective witnesses for Christ to the world.

Week 9

Personal Application

Special Scriptures

INTIMACY

A. Covenant: The Basis for True Intimacy with God.

1. Produces life, spiritually, soulishly, physically [John 10:10; Romans 8:11].

2. Spiritual purity is required for spiritual intimacy.
   a. Only available through the shed blood of Jesus. [Hebrews 9:22, 12:24].
   b. Jesus has provided the ONLY means to intimacy with God.
   c. Covenant must be entered into for true intimacy.

3. Satan's counterfeits.
   a. Satan has falsely promised all kinds of avenues into intimacy with God.
      1) Religions, cults, communing with nature, meditation, etc.
      2) Everyone of them misses the vital element of covenant relationship through the blood of Jesus.
   b. God's plan cannot be duplicated.

B. Covenant Is Also the Basis for Intimacy Between Husband and Wife.

1. God's Design: Under Covenant Covering
   a. Commitment and protection of covenant allows couple to be totally vulnerable to each other [Genesis 2:24,25].
   b. Man and woman were designed both physically and emotionally to experience great pleasure and satisfaction from sexual union.

2. Intimacy Produces Life.
   a. In Song of Solomon, references to fruit, gardens, and vineyards are used in conjunction with the relationship between the lover and his beloved.
   b. Sexual union as God created it is not self-centered nor self-seeking.
      1) It is refreshing and energizing.
      2) It produces a desire to give more than receive.
   c. Children are natural examples of the life-giving aspect of our sexual union [Genesis 1:28; Malachi 2:15].
   d. Read Song of Solomon together to see the beauty of sexual union as God created it.
      1) Sexual union was God's gift to Adam and Eve in the Garden [Genesis 1:28,31].
      2) It is also His special wedding gift to each couple that enters into His covenant plan for marriage [1 Corinthians 7:3-5].

3. Physical purity is required for physical intimacy.
   a. You can tell how important something is to the heart of God by how much time the enemy spends perverting it.
   b. Satan has spent much time counterfeiting the intimacy of sexual union.
      1) Just as with spiritual counterfeits to imitate spiritual intimacy, Satan has also fabricated sexual counterfeits to imitate sexual intimacy (masturbation, homosexuality, fornication, adultery, incest, etc.)
      2) Do not produce sexual intimacy and are damaging counterfeits [Romans 1:24-27].
   c. Many are not able to experience sexual intimacy as God intends because of the wounding of sexual sin.
   d. Sexual union without covenant covering permits vulnerability with no protection.
      1) Strips the ability to be intimate.

Personal Application

Special Scriptures

tear down the walls

fake intimacy

INTIMACY

        2) Instead of edifying and ministering, it degrades and defiles.
        3) Instead of enhancing, it diminishes [Proverbs 6:32,33].
    e. No wonder scripture tells us that one who commits sexual sin, sins against his own body [1 Corinthians 6:18].

C. Effects of Sexual Sin.
    1. Man was created to be tender toward and understanding of his wife [1 Peter 3:7].
        a. Jesus is the example of the intimate Husband.
            1) He overwhelmingly loves His bride.
            2) It is easy for us to respond to His love.
        b. When a man sins sexually, his heart is hardened.
            1) He uses, not enhances, a woman.
            2) A tender heart cannot endure the ravages of sexual sin.
        c. A man's callused, hardened heart often manifests in lust, not love, towards his wife.
            1) He cannot love his wife the way God intends.
            2) He can only show affection or interest when he wants to have sex.
            3) When he looks at wife or touches her, she feels defiled.
            4) Once his heart is hardened in sexual sin, only God can soften it again [Ezekiel 36:26].
            5) No counterfeit of Satan's will enable him to love as God intended.
    2. Woman was created to respond to the love of the man to whom she is married [Ephesians 5:22].
        a. In response to his love, she gives herself totally to her husband.
            1) He loves and enhances that which she has entrusted to him.
            2) What she gives is returned to her in greater fullness so she responds again with greater love.
            3) A woman who is cherished usually has no problem loving and giving in return.
        b. When a woman sins sexually, what she gives is not returned to her.
            1) In counterfeit relationships, there is no enhancement of that which she has given.
            2) An emptiness develops within her and she cannot seem to find fulfillment.
        c. This often manifests in insecurity and poor self-image.
            1) She may not be able to respond to her husband physically.
                a) She may expect her husband to fulfill her deep inner emptiness.
                b) She feels he doesn't love her or meet her needs.
            ✶ 2) <u>Only Jesus can fill that void</u> and give her the peace and fulfillment she desires.

    3. Men and women wounded by sexual sin may <u>seek fulfillment in compulsive behaviors</u> with alcohol, drugs, food, gambling, or multiple sexual partners.
        a. Each time the disappointment is greater, though, and fulfillment slips farther away [Proverbs 14:12].
        b. Just as spiritual purity is the basis for spiritual intimacy, so sexual purity is the basis for sexual intimacy.
        ✶ c. If you have lost that purity, Jesus longs to restore it to you.

    4. If you entered marriage sexually pure, your sexual intimacy should be able to deepen as the years go by.
        a. Purity is sometimes maintained through fear or distrust of intimacy.

Week 10

Personal Application

Special Scriptures

Heart like a piece of paper
  each 1st given away isn't returned to you

INTIMACY

   b. This may keep people out of sexual sin before marriage, but it does not contribute to sexual intimacy after marriage.

D. Healing From the Wounding of Sexual Sin.

 1. God, who designed sexual intimacy, has redeemed us from the curse of sin and death [Romans 8:2].
  a. If you feel sex is dirty or if you fear enjoying it, Jesus longs to heal that wounding.
  b. He wants you to enjoy the fulfillment God has designed for you.

 2. *"Marriage is honorable among all, and the bed undefiled"* [Hebrews 13:4 NKJV].

E. Steps to Take to Be Healed from the Wounding of Sexual Sin.

 1. **Repent.**
  a. Of all sexual sins you have committed.
   1) Before your marriage.
   2) Outside of your marriage.
   3) Any perverted sexual activity, whether before or during your marriage.
  b. Justification of sin only perpetuates the consequences.
  c. If you are not sure if something was sin or if scripture does not specifically mention it, ask the following questions:
   1) Did it edify?
   2) Did one or both partners feel defiled?
   3) Was there disagreement whether it was right or not?
  d. Lusting in your heart is sin [Matthew 5:28].
   1) You may even have lusted toward your spouse.
   2) Ask God to teach you how to truly love your spouse.
  e. When you have repented for all sexual sin, receive not only the **forgiveness** of Jesus but also the **cleansing of His blood** [1 John 1:9].
   1) It is the blood of Jesus that washes away the defilement of sin.
   2) Receive from Jesus the **restoration of your innocence** [Psalm 51:10].

 2. **Forgive.**
  a. Anyone who has wounded or used you sexually, whether consensual or not.
   1) Through incest or rape, premarital sex or adultery, fondling or petting, exposure.
   2) May have been a lover, a former spouse, a relative or friend, or even your spouse who related to you in lust, not love.
  b. Forgive them and release them to Jesus.
  c. **Forgive yourself**, whether you were a willing partner or an innocent victim.
   1) Forgive yourself for the defilement.
   2) Begin to love yourself as Jesus loves you. You are precious to Him.

 3. **Sever all ungodly soul ties.**
  a. Anytime the mind, will, and emotions are deeply involved in a relationship, a soul tie is formed.
  b. Soul ties hold us mentally and emotionally to previous relationships and people.
  c. They can be formed under favorable conditions as well as unfavorable conditions.
   1) An example of a favorable condition is 1 Samuel 18:1.
   2) An example of an unfavorable condition is Genesis 34:2,3,8.

Week 10

Personal Application

Special Scriptures

INTIMACY

        d. Need to break all soul ties that bind you to a previous relationship.
            1) Whether you consented or not.
            2) This includes previous spouses.
        e. Severing soul ties does not necessarily mean ending the relationship.
            1) You may continue to relate, for example, to a previous spouse.
            2) The emotional and mental ties will be broken, though.

    4. **Take authority over demonic spirits** given access through sin [Romans 6:16].
        a. They create areas of demonic hold.
            1) Areas in which you simply cannot maintain victory.
            2) This is not a case of not trying; you are driven in this area.
        b. Spiritual assignments can bring forth lust, shame, promiscuity, impotence, frigidity and many more.
        c. Ask Holy Spirit to reveal to you any spiritual assignments and take authority over them in Jesus' name.
        d. Break any generational patterns.
            1) Take authority over assignments against your children and down through the generations.
            2) If these assignments are not canceled in Jesus' name, the sin may be repeated from generation to generation.
            3) Do the same for adopted children with different generational backgrounds.
                a) Often they have been conceived in fornication.
                b) If you do not break the assignments against them, they may struggle with the same demonic strongholds.
                c) You can set them free in Jesus' name.

    5. After you have dealt with each of these areas, you have been set free in Jesus.
        a. Are on the way to the healing of your sexual union as husband and wife.
            1) Realize that sexual healing is not accomplished overnight.
            2) The sin was removed as soon as you confessed it [1 John 1:9].
            3) Scars take some time to heal.
        b. Be patient with each other during the time of healing.
            1) Performance is the devil's measure of sexual fulfillment [2 Corinthians 10:12].
                a) It is self-centered and self-directed.
                b) God gave your sex drive for the fulfillment of your spouse, not you.
            2) Begin to see your love making as a time to minister to each other.
                a) Get the focus off "me and my needs" and onto your spouse.
                b) Do not do anything that would wound or defile your spouse.
            3) Pray together in the spirit before making love.
                a) Ask God to bless your union as He did Adam and Eve's [Genesis 1:28].
                b) Recognize that He is part of your sexual union.
        c. Refuse condemnation regarding previous sexual relationships because they are now under the blood of Jesus [Romans 8:1].

F. Maintaining Victory.

    1. To maintain your victory and obtain total healing, you must keep yourself from impurity and renew your mind with the Word of God [Romans 12:1,2].
        a. Your mind is the battleground where the enemy attempts to regain what he lost.

Week 10

Personal Application

Special Scriptures

INTIMACY

            1) Guard yourselves from the worldly image of sexual lust.
            2) Refuse the message fed through pornography, soap operas, romance novels, the internet, etc.
        b. Renew your mind (replace the old thought patterns with the Word of God.)
            1) You have the mind of Christ [1 Corinthians 2:16].
            2) Refuse the enemy's thoughts.

2. Guard your sexual union together as husband and wife.
    a. Lock your shields of faith together over your point of wounding.
        1) Examples: If one spouse has a problem with lust, give him or her permission to share whenever tempted or if one spouse was a victim of incest or rape, give permission to share when tempted with shame.
        2) Don't take that as an admission of failure.
        3) Lock your shields of faith together for protection against the enemy.
    b. Stand united as a one-flesh team in the power of Jesus [1 Corinthians 10:12,13].

3. Be led of the Spirit in all things [Romans 8:14], including your sexual union.
    a. Usually we are led by passion (flesh) or feelings (soul).
        1) The Holy Spirit gives direction before and after we are married to keep us in God's will.
        2) If we have learned to hear His voice before marriage, we know how to hear Him after.
    b. Usually we have not sought His guidance regarding our sexual union.
        1) We need to become attentive to His voice.
        2) He will minister to us through our sexual union if we are obedient.

4. Make sure you take time to minister to each other sexually.
    a. Don't get so busy there's no time for making love.
    b. Don't become "so spiritual" that you don't have a physical relationship.
    c. God commands couples to have a sexual relationship [1 Corinthians 7:3-4].
        1) This one aspect makes marriage different than any other relationship.
        2) God will minister to you through a healthy sexual union.
        3) Without sexual union, marriage is vulnerable to enemy attack [1 Corinthians 7:5].
    d. If your sexual relationship needs healing:
        1) Allow God to regenerate "courting."
            a) Develop a renewed appreciation and respect for each other.
            b) As these are developed, love and desire will follow.
        2) Give each other time to grow in sexual love [Song of Sol. 2:7; 3:5; 8:4].
        3) Submit yourselves to Jesus, allow Him to put desire for each other back in your hearts, and be obedient to His directions.

5. Our approach to sexual intimacy influences our children.
    a. We must not convey to them that sex is bad to keep them from sin.
    b. Teach them honestly regarding the fulfillment of sexual intimacy along with the reasons for God's commandments.
        1) They will be better equipped to enter marriage pure and with a healthy attitude toward sex.
        2) The wounding of sexual sin need not be repeated in the next generation.
            a) Wisdom and knowledge of the Word of God will prepare them.
            b) Our obedience will be their example.

Week 10

Personal Application

Special Scriptures

SPIRITUAL WARFARE

A. Creation of One-Flesh Team.

   1. God placed within both man and woman abilities.
      a. When combined they are an unbeatable warfare team.
      b. The fall handicapped one-flesh warfare, but through Jesus the ability was restored.

   2. Consider everything taught in this lesson from the standpoint of one-flesh team warfare.
      a. Most families have only one spouse who does warfare.
      b. No wonder there are casualties.
      c. If you are not fighting the enemy together, you are wasting precious resources.
      d. Let this be a time of the Lord teaching both spouses how to war together.

B. We Have Same Abilities Placed in Adam and Eve.

   1. The Fall perverted the outflow.

   2. "Helper Suitable" ("help meet" in KJV).
      a. Comes from Hebrew root word meaning "to surround."
      b. Used numerous times in Old Testament.
         1) Only twice as "helper suitable" or "help meet"
            a) Both in reference to creation of Eve.
            b) Genesis 2:18,20.
         2) All other times it is used as "help" or "aid"
            a) Used in reference to the Lord.
            b) Refers to Him as a "help" or "aid" to Israel.
      c. God gave clever strategies to Israel to gain victories.
         1) Sometimes the Israelites did not even have to fight.
         2) God's help saved a great deal of casualties.

   3. God placed within woman a similar ability to assist in battle.
      a. We have labeled it "radar".
      b. It is an inner knowing that senses enemy attack.
      c. God placed it in woman to detect enemy activity at a distance.
      d. It is one aspect of "suitable helper".

   4. God gave Adam a corresponding warrior ability.
      a. In Adam's heart, God placed a desire to win.
      b. Adam was created in the image of God--he was the very best!
      c. God's desire was for Adam to triumph over the enemy.
      d. The approach of the enemy would alert that warrior quality and Adam would rise up in authority, knowing that he had the victory.

   5. Perversion of abilities.
      a. Satan's attack:
         1) His first strategy was to knock out the radar.
            a) "...has God indeed said...?" [Genesis 3:1]
            b) The diversion worked, the radar failed and Eve was deceived [2 Corinthians 11:3; 1 Timothy 2:14].

Personal Application

Special Scriptures

SPIRITUAL WARFARE

        2) His second strategy was to defeat the warrior [Genesis 3:6].
           a) Adam failed to exercise his authority over the enemy.
           b) He disobeyed God, and ate of the Tree of the Knowledge of Good and Evil.
    b. Effects of the Fall on the Radar (Wife).
        1) Radar fails to just pick up spiritual discernment.
           a) Now picks up everything (like snow on a radar screen).
           b) Things of the flesh (fear, suspicion, criticism, worry, and anxiety) get mixed in with spiritual discernment.
        2) Instead of encouraging her husband, nagging and aggression are often an outflow of the overload.
    c. Affects of the Fall on the Warrior (Husband).
        1) Now fights to excel over men, not spiritual enemy.
           a) Competition and greed have replaced spiritual superiority.
           b) Men fight against men in sports arena and work place.
        2) Husband may tune out wife instead of listening to her, abandoning her to enemy attack.
    d. Time to resurrect godly qualities.
        1) When both spouses are functioning as created, the home is impervious to enemy attack.
        2) Rise up and be what you were created to be.
        3) These qualities will need fine-tuning and sharpening.
           a) Pray together daily and learn to separate spiritual from carnal.
           b) Husband must help wife to discern between fleshly anxiety and spiritual alerting.
           c) Wife must call on husband when under attack and help him to rise up in battle.

C. Protection of God.

  1. God has provided armor for our protection in battle.
    a. Remember daily that you have it on; never take it off.
    b. Remind children they are wearing it.
    c. Wearing your armor well means walking in the fullness of what each piece means.

  2. Armor of God [Ephesians 6:11, 13-18].
    a. Helmet of Salvation.
        1) Covers your mind and protects your thoughts.
        2) See through Jesus' eyes and hear with Jesus' ears.
    b. Breastplate of Righteousness.
        1) Covers your heart [Proverbs 4:23].
        2) Only the righteousness of Jesus can change hearts.
    c. Loins girded with Truth.
        1) Loins are life-giving parts.
        2) Truth of the Word gives life.
    d. Feet shod with the preparation of the Gospel of Peace.
        1) Always be ready to take gospel forth.
        2) Peace undisturbed by unexpected requests from God.
    e. Take up the Shield of Faith.
        1) Faith protects you against circumstances.

Week 11

Personal Application

Special Scriptures

SPIRITUAL WARFARE

            2) Ward off doubt and fear.
- f. Take up the Sword of the Spirit.
    1) Sword = Word of God.
    2) You must be in Word daily.
    3) It is an offensive as well as defensive weapon.
    4) Must be in your heart and in your mouth [Deuteronomy 30:14].
- g. Pray always in the spirit.
    1) Sow to the spirit, not the flesh [Romans 8:5].
    2) Keeps you in constant contact with your Commander-in-Chief for instructions.

D. Other Assets Given to Us in Battle.

1. Authority in Jesus' name.
    a. All authority in heaven and on earth has been given to Jesus [Matthew 28:18]
    b. Asking in His name [John 14:13 NIV].
    c. Binding (to forbid, prohibit, declare to be illicit) and loosing in His name [Matthew 18:18 NIV].

2. There is power in the blood of Jesus.
    a. Blood must be shed for forgiveness of sin [Hebrews 9:22, 26 NIV].
    b. The Blood of Jesus overcomes the enemy [Revelation 12:11 NIV].
    c. Once we have received Jesus as Lord and Savior, the blood of Jesus is at work in our lives.
    d. Blood of Jesus was shed for people, not animals and things.
        1) As you pray, cover people with the blood for protection.
        2) Ask protection for animals and possessions because they are covered under our covenant with the Lord.
            a) God watches over and protects those in covenant with Him [Job 1:10].
            b) Jesus asked the Father's protection for us [John 17:11].

3. Praise.
    a. The Lord inhabits the praises of His people [Psalm 22:3].
    b. The enemy is silenced by praise [Psalm 8:2 NIV].
    c. Praise God frequently.
        1) It is a powerful weapon.
        2) He is worthy of our praise.

E. We Have the Advantage of Weapons.

1. Our Weapons.
    a. *"For the weapons of our warfare are not carnal but mighty in God for pulling down strongholds, casting down arguments and every high thing that exalts itself against the knowledge of God bringing every thought into captivity to the obedience of Christ, and being ready to punish all disobedience when your obedience is fulfilled"* [2 Corinthians 10:4-6 NKJV].
        1) Although we are human, we do not fight with human weapons.
        2) Our weapons are empowered of God and are supernatural in nature.
            a) Deuteronomy 33:27.
            b) Zechariah 4:6.

Week 11

Personal Application

Special Scriptures

SPIRITUAL WARFARE

           3) God's plan is for us to overcome the enemy because He has overcome him.
               a) John 16:33.
               b) 1 John 4:4.
               c) Romans 16:20
       b. Our victory does not depend upon our own ability.

   2. Enemy's Weapons.
       a. Enemy wages war on the saints [Revelation 19:19].
           1) War is continuous.
           2) He is dedicated to our destruction [John 10:10].
       b. Weapons are limited.
       ※c. *"No temptation has overtaken you except such as is common to man; but God is faithful, who will not allow you to be tempted beyond what you are able, but with the temptation will also make the <u>way of escape,</u> that you may be able to bear it"* [1 Corinthians.10:13 NKJV].
           1) Enemy's weapons are common to man (carnal).
           2) They are limited in power.
           3) God has promised a way out with each one (easily defensible).
       d. Appeals to the flesh.
           1) Romans 8:5,6.
           2) Galatians 5:19-21.
           3) Galatians 6:8
       e. Creates strife and division.
           1) James 3:16.
           2) James 4:1-3.

   3. Stay in the spirit when fighting the enemy.
       a. Our weapons are stronger in the spirit; we always win.
       b. Our enemy is craftier in the flesh; he has the upper hand there.

   4. With superior weapons and the protection of God, why do we fail?

F. Vigilance.

   1. Must be self-controlled and alert [1 Peter 5:8 NIV].

   2. As a one-flesh team, patrol your hedge daily [Job 1:10].
       ※a. Must check for enemy entrances.
       ※b. Know the condition of all that God has entrusted [Proverbs 27:23 NIV].

   3. Two types of battle.
       a. Defensive.
           ※1) Regaining territory. w/ children
           2) Spy out the Land [Numbers 13:17].
       b. Offensive.
           1) Intercede to know the enemy's plans ahead of time.
           2) See what lies ahead.

   4. Recognizing the enemy [1 John 4:1 KJV].
       a. Test the spirits.
       b. Check out what is coming your way.

WEEK 11

PERSONAL APPLICATION

SPECIAL SCRIPTURES

use as example
tell our children

SPIRITUAL WARFARE

G. Enemy Identification.

[handwritten margin note: remind us + children]

1. Enemy is not our:
   a. Spouse.
   b. Children.
   c. Brothers and sisters in the Lord/Boss/Etc.
2. The enemy has highly organized forces opposing the army of God.
   a. *"For we wrestle not against flesh and blood, but against principalities, against powers, against the rulers of the darkness of this world, against spiritual wickedness in high places"* [Ephesians 6:12 KJV].
      1) Principalities.
         a) Greek = arche.
         b) Means "chief ranking."
         c) Those in highest authority in Satan's forces.
      2) Powers.
         a) Greek = exousia.
         b) Means "delegated authority" or "jurisdiction."
         c) Demonic forces given power over certain portions of the earth.
      3) Rulers.
         a) Greek = kosmokrator.
         b) Means "ruler in this world."
         c) Demons assigned to influence world rulers.
      4) Spiritual wickedness.
         a) Greek = poneria.
         b) Means "depravity".
         c) Lowest ranking and most numerous of demonic forces.
   b. Ask the Holy Spirit for discernment when you wage spiritual warfare.
      1) Is it spiritual wickedness or are you up against one of the rulers or powers?
      2) Is it something just affecting your family or are you battling a ruling spirit over your part of the nation?
      3) Get specific by the Holy Spirit's direction and target the correct source of demonic activity.

H. One-Flesh Team Warfare.

1. Don't allow the enemy to divide the two of you.
   a. Your unity is the key to successful spiritual warfare.
   b. Ask the Holy Spirit to teach you how to flow together.

2. Synergistic power. *"Five of you shall chase a hundred, and a hundred of you shall put ten thousand to flight; your enemies shall fall before you by the sword"* [Leviticus 26:8].
   a. Your power increases exponentially.
   b. It is well worth the time and effort it takes to learn.

PERSONAL APPLICATION

Connected - finally time about Satanic bible → experience in room

SPECIAL SCRIPTURES

LIFE PATTERNS

A. It Is Time to Examine Life Patterns

1. Recognition.
   a. It is like looking at a painting, up close, section by section and then stepping back to look at the whole picture.
      1) Can only see brush strokes and lines close up.
      2) You have been examining segments of married life for past eleven weeks.
   b. Now it is time to take a look at the whole picture.

2. Definition of Life Patterns.
   a. Patterns of thinking and acting shaped within us throughout our life.
   b. Sometimes we form our own.
   c. Sometimes they are handed down through generations.
      1) Biblical example: Deceit - Abraham (lied about Sarah being his sister); continued with his son, Isaac (lied about his wife being his sister); continued in his son, Jacob (pretended to be his brother Esau and took his blessing); continued in Jacob's family (brothers sold Joseph into slavery and told father he had been killed).
      2) May be caused by what many in the Body of Christ call "generational influences" [Exodus 20:5,6].
   d. Patterns are sometimes difficult to see.
      1) Sometimes they need to be pointed out to us.
      2) Do you know what this says?

      3) We need to learn to see light against the background of darkness.
      4) Once we have recognized what is written, it will be easily identified when seen again.
   e. Life patterns are the same way.
      1) Need light of the Word to shine against darkness.
         a) *"God is light and in Him is no darkness at all"* [I John 1:5].
         b) We need to see things as God sees them, not with natural eyes.
      2) Once recognized, have no problem seeing again.

B. Recognizing Life Patterns.

1. Godly.
   a. They match up with the Word.
   b. Look for these - don't concentrate only on the negatives.
   c. Become aware of the godly principles in practice in your marriage.
      1) Often "good" marriages are unaware of what they have done to succeed.
      2) You have now been shown the principles that you have followed from the Word.
      3) You can now share these principles with other marriages to reproduce the life you have been given.
   d. You need to cultivate and continue godly patterns.

Personal Application

Special Scriptures

LIFE PATTERNS

   2. Ungodly.
      a. The standard is God's Word, not what we think is right or wrong.
         1) Bank tellers are taught to recognize counterfeit money by being shown real money.
         2) Become so familiar with the truth of the Word that you will know what is counterfeit [1 John 2:20,21].
         3) Any pattern that does not measure up to the Word is ungodly.
      b. May be generational.
         1) Observe if the pattern is also present in relatives.
         2) Ask the Holy Spirit to identify generational influences, if any.
         3) Take authority over them in Jesus' name and break their hold on your family [Leviticus 26:40,42; 1 Peter 1:18,19].

   3. The Word of God is the standard.
      a. Scriptural principles have been taught for the past eleven weeks.
         1) Each week leadership shared godly patterns from the Word and showed, with examples from their own lives, how they did or did not match up.
         2) You will need each of the scriptural principles shared to change ungodly life patterns in your marriage.
      b. God's Word is the standard for change [2 Timothy 3:16].
         1) It is important that you understand each scriptural principle you have studied and know how to apply it to your own marriage.
         2) Each one builds on the other.
         3) If you have had difficulty with any one area, you need to go back and continue to work on it.
         4) This is an ongoing, lifetime project [Philippians 3:12-17].
      c. The Word exposes life patterns.
         1) It gives the goal.
         2) It provides the way to go from darkness to light [Psalm 18:28; Job 12:22].

C. Changing Ungodly Patterns.

   1. Jesus redeemed our marriage back to the life Adam and Eve had in their marriage.
      a. Jesus is life-giving.
      b. Our covenant with Jesus affords us a victorious life [1 Corinthians 15:57].
         1) Jesus is life-giving [John 10:10 KJV].
         2) We are to reign in this life through Jesus [Romans 5:17 NKJV].
      c. Adam and Eve had no sin (darkness) between them.
         1) There was no sin, no shame between them [Genesis 2:25].
         2) When sin entered they covered themselves from each other [Genesis 3:7].
      d. There is to be no sin (shame) between us as husband and wife.
         1) We are not to cover ourselves from each other.
         2) We are to be open and honest with each other.

   2. We are commanded to be the light of the world [Matthew 5:14,16].
      a. If there is sin (darkness) between us, our light cannot shine as God desires.
         1) Sin causes us to put our light under a bushel.

Week 12

Personal Application

Special Scriptures

LIFE PATTERNS

        2) Sin is not just a private matter; it affects our spouse, our family, and the rest of the body of Christ.
- b. Sin is contrary to our relationship with God [Romans 6:11].
- c. We can and must get rid of all sin in our lives [1 John 1:9].
  1) Overt sin.
     - a) Areas where "we just can't stop."
     - b) "Little" sins that "don't really matter to God."
     - c) When we know we are sinning, but God "loves us anyway."
     - d) It is God's grace at work within us that enables us to overcome areas of sin in our lives.
  2) Hidden sin [Mark 4:22].
     - a) Private sins where we cannot seem to get victory.
     - b) Sins we have confessed to God but not to our spouse.
     - c) Past sins we fear our spouse will discover.

3. Repent of (turn away from) all sin [1 John 1:9].
   - a. Past.
     1) Non repented, deeply buried, highly sensitive areas.
     2) Sin continues to have a hold until exposed to the light, through repentance.
   - b. Ongoing.
     1) Private little areas we don't think Jesus can handle.
     2) Saying "God can't help me" is pride.
     3) God will give the strength to resist the enemy when we submit ourselves to Him [James 4:7].
   - c. Things God has convicted us of during the past eleven weeks, but we have defended (justified).
     1) Repentance breaks the cycle of the old sin patterns but justification just keeps them going.
     2) Don't hold out on God [1 John 1:8].
     3) God wants us to walk totally free in every area of our lives [Galatians 5:1].

4. Exposing sin between spouses [James 5:16].
   - a. Sin hidden from our spouse causes a distortion in the way we relate.
     1) We cannot be naked and unashamed (open) with sin between us.
     2) We are always fearful our spouse will find out.
     3) We must continue deception (which is sin) to keep the sin hidden.
   - b. We often fear exposure will wound our spouse.
     1) Our spouse was already wounded when the sin occurred.
        - a) Remember we are one-flesh; there is nothing that we do that does not affect our spouse.
        - b) Sin separates us from each other.
     2) Fear, doubt, and suspicion arise.
     3) In the body, an abscess has to be lanced (cut open, exposing and draining the festering infection) for healing to take place.
     4) Sin between spouses must be treated the same way.
   - c. Do not "dump" your confession on your spouse.

Week 12

Personal Application

Special Scriptures

LIFE PATTERNS

            1) Pray for God's timing.
            2) Pray to prepare your spouse to receive.
            3) Be led of the Spirit.
            4) Don't try to "pry sin out" of your spouse.

        d. It is Jesus that gives the direction and He (Jesus) is the one breaking down the barrier of the dividing wall between the two of you, thus making you one [Ephesians 2:14,15].

        e. James 5:16 gives the result: of confessing our sin *"...so that you may be healed."*
            1) Allow the Holy Spirit time for comforting and healing.
                a) The spouse confessing usually feels relieved to "get it off his or her chest."
                b) The spouse hearing the confession must begin his or her own healing process.
            2) Tears are a part of healing and soften the sinner's heart.
                a) Do not reject your spouse for crying.
                b) Allow the tears to break the hardness of your heart as you see the affects of your sin.
            3) Don't allow self-pity if you are the offended spouse.
                a) True tears are healing.
                b) Do not use tears as a means of manipulation.
            4) Realize that sin hurts (puts in bondage) more the one who sins than the spouse who has been sinned against.
            5) Both spouses must be led of the Spirit for healing to be completed.

    5. Forgiveness is the key to healing.
        a. Forgive your spouse.
        b. Forgive your relatives who have perpetuated the generational sin.
        c. Give yourself grace because Jesus has forgiven you.

    6. Lock shields together over the point of wounding.
        a. Don't allow devil to divide the two of you and conquer ever again.
        b. Every sin has two-sided consequences.
        c. Help protect each other from future sin.
        d. The enemy attack is against your one-flesh.

D. Maintaining Godly Patterns.

    1. Establish patterns on the Word.

    2. Pray together daily.
        a. Set a time together.
        b. It is better to have a <u>consistent, shorter</u> time than inconsistent longer one.

    3. Have no hidden sin between you.
        a. Be quick to repent.
        b. Forgive your spouse quickly.
        c. Be open, honest, and transparent with each other.

    4. Obedience is key.

Week 12

Personal Application

Special Scriptures

LIFE PATTERNS

       a. Obey the Word.
       b. Obey the direction of the Holy Spirit.
          1) Resolve to obey instantly each instruction God gives you.
          2) Consistent obedience will improve your ability to hear directions from God.
       c. Repent if you miss His direction and/or do your own thing.
          1) God has no Plan B.
          2) When we repent of having missed His plan for us, He makes a new Plan A for us.
          3) He is 100% for our success in His plan for us.

E. In Summary, the Word:

    1. Enables us to recognize and expose ungodly life patterns in our lives.

    2. Shows us the godly patterns we should be living continuously.

    3. Shows us how to change our ungodly life patterns into godly ones.

F. Marriage Ministries International Vision - Powerhouse homes.

    1. Light can shine forth from our home when no darkness between us [Romans 13:12].
       a. Out of our darkness, Jesus shines His light in our hearts. [2 Corinthians 4:5,6].
       b. We are to bring the knowledge of the glory of God to others.
       c. That is the whole point of a powerhouse home.

    2. Our homes can shine brightly to others when we have no hidden sin in our own lives [Ephesians 5:8-11].
       a. The devil has no hold to keep us back.
       b. Condemnation has no place in us [Romans 8:1].

    3. Power resides in unity, not division.
       a. Matthew 12:25.
       b. We must be united in Christ giving no place to the devil.
          1) We have been set free by the shed blood of Jesus.
          2) We need to walk in that freedom.
       c. The unity and power of our covenant with Jesus, and with each other in Him, is the basis for the powerhouse home that *multiplies* our power [Leviticus 26:8].

Week 12

Personal Application

Special Scriptures

ONE-FLESH MINISTRY

A. God's Plan for Your Marriage.

1. God's Word never fails.
   a. The tools you have received will accomplish miraculous change in your marriage when applied correctly.
   b. God has not given you all this so that only your marriage be blessed.
      1) He has deposited much in you that could help others.
      2) It is His desire that you reach out and bless others [John 15:16].

2. Bear Fruit and Multiply.
   a. Three times in Genesis 1, God speaks of bearing fruit with seed in it.
      1) Genesis 1:11.
      2) Genesis 1:12.
      3) Genesis 1:29.
   b. Two other times He speaks of bearing fruit and multiplying.
      1) Genesis 1:22.
      2) Genesis 1:28.
   c. God's plan from the beginning of creation is that we produce fruit with the seed of reproducibility in it.
      1) Fruit we produce is not only for our own lives but also for the lives of others into whom we sow.
      2) Fruit with seed in it will enable them to sow also.

3. The Three Seasons.
   a. *"This year you will eat what grows by itself, and the second year what springs from that. But in the third year sow and reap, plant vineyards and eat their fruit"* [Isaiah 37:30].
   b. The First Season.
      1) The beginning of the Christian walk.
      2) We eat *"what grows by itself."*
      3) Self-focused season in which our goal is to receive spiritual feeding.
      4) As with a new-born baby, God intends for others to care for us and feed us from the Word.
      5) We receive what comes our way without much effort to seek specific feeding.
   c. The Second Season.
      1) We eat *"what springs from that."*
      2) A bit more selective, we begin seeking the Lord diligently regarding what church to attend and what teachings to receive.
      3) Still somewhat self-directed but may reach out to others.
      4) Can be compared to gleaning a field; there is plenty to eat but we must put forth some effort to receive it.
   d. The Third Season.
      1) We must *"sow and reap, plant vineyards and eat their fruit."*
      2) No longer is our feeding based solely on the labor of others.
      3) No longer are we able to passively expect others to care for us.
      4) We must now sow and reap in order to be fed.

Personal Application

New Plan A
use tools — Strife breaks
(i.e.) agreement

Special Scriptures

ONE-FLESH MINISTRY

  e.   If fail to recognize the third season's requirements:
    1)   Will make such comments as, "This pastor just doesn't feed me the way he used to," or "Christianity just seems boring to me."
     a)   Pastor or anyone never again will feed us as they did in the first and second seasons.
     b)   Now feeding depends on our own sowing and reaping. *[Heb 5:12]*
    2)   We are required to *"plant vineyards;"* that is, produce more fruit than we can personally consume so we can give to others.
    3)   We do get to *"eat their fruit"* but others, not ourselves, are to become our focus.
  f.   If one refuses to sow and reap:
    1)   Will spiritually starve and eventually may fall away from the faith.
    2)   Will become a beggar at the banquet table of others.
     a)   Spiritual beggars go from person to person draining each of their resources.
     b)   They are always angry with the previous feeder who never quite met their needs.
     c)   They will tell you that no one else has been able to help them and you are God's answer for them.
     d)   A few months at your table and they will leave for another one, having exhausted you and your patience.

4.   What Season are You in Now?
  a.   If you are in the First or Second Season:
    1)   God has planned them for you as a special time of receiving.
    2)   Receive the fullness of what God has for you now and store your spiritual seed for the coming season.
  b.   If you are in the Third Season:
    1)   The time has come for you to sow and reap and give out from what God has given you.
    2)   Are you bored with Christianity and having trouble finding teachings that bless you? *[Quiz → Gem Season]*
     a)   You have entered a season where in order to be blessed you must bless others.
     b)   This does not mean that you will never again be fed by other's teachings.
     c)   You will be blessed by them again as you give out of the abundance you have received [Matthew 10:8; Luke 6:38].
    3)   Are you eager to give out from what God has given you but just aren't sure how to do it?
     a)   The Lord will give you direction as you seek Him.
     b)   He wants you to sow and reap even more than you do.

Personal Application

→ need to give more

Special Scriptures

Week 13

ONE-FLESH MINISTRY

        c. We are a fat church.
           1) Our first and second seasons are filled with abundant ministry and blessings.
           2) Do we enter the third season with a desire to feed others or to continue to feed ourselves?
        d. What season are you in now? If the third, it's time to give out!

    5. Just as God blessed Adam and Eve and gave them an assignment [Genesis 1:28] He has a specific plan for you as a one-flesh team and for your marriage [Jeremiah 29:11].
        a. It was assigned the day you were married.
        b. It is God's will that your marriage be strong so you reach out in His name.
        c. When God created Adam and Eve and gave them to each other, He immediately gave them an assignment to accomplish.
           1) God also has an assignment for you.
               a) In your local church or within your community.
               b) Within a ministry.
           2) Fulfilling your assignment is important:
               a) To God.
               b) To others.
               c) To yourselves.
               d) You are called according to His purpose [Romans 8:28].
           3) You may already know what it is or may still be seeking His will.
           4) You need to walk in the fullness of one-flesh to accomplish your assignment.
           5) Your home should be the powerhouse that God described in the vision of Marriage Ministries International.

B. Preparation for the Assignment.

    1. If you believe you are in your first or second season and are not functioning in fullness of one-flesh consider continuing through another Married for Life home group.
        a. Submitting to Him together, enables Him to mold us and blend us as He desires [Romans 8:26-29].
        b. Scriptural principles will be reinforced, enabling you to walk in greater unity and strength.
        c. Attending a different group gives the opportunity to experience more than one leadership couple and teaching style.
        d. Even if you have applied yourselves well, often only surface work is completed in a marriage the first time in Married for Life.

    2. Many couples need a structure in which to work.
        a. Married for Life home groups provide structure and support.
        b. Whether you continue in another group or not, allow the Lord to continue doing a deeper and deeper work in your marriage.
        c. As you as a couple grow and strengthen as one, you will be better equipped to reach out to others.

Personal Application

Special Scriptures

I know the plans I have for you...

Re read the vision

ONE-FLESH MINISTRY

C. Determining your call [Ephesians 2:10].

1. Seek the Lord for His call on your lives. *Prayer*

2. Ask yourselves some questions:
    a. Where is your burden?
        1) Young people? or Older people?
        2) Singles? Or Marrieds?
    b. Burden to:
        1) Heal?
        2) Strengthen?
    c. Do you function better: Nurturing, one-to-one relationship? Teaching larger groups?
    d. Does your heart cry out to: Retrieve the lost? Strengthen the saved?
    e. Do you have a burden for children?
    f. What is your geographical burden?
        1) Church? Neighborhood?
        2) City? State?
        3) A portion of this country? Another country?

3. Usually the desire of your heart is what you have been called to do.
    a. Remember you are called as one-flesh.
        1) God will give each spouse specifics of the call.
        2) Blend the specifics together for the total call.
    b. Initially burdens may be based on your own need for ministry.
        1) Allow God to minister to you and heal you.
        2) As you are healed, your burden may change.
        3) His call on your one-flesh team will become more and more fine-tuned.
    c. It is important to seek Him together as one-flesh.

4. Seek God for instructions for carrying out your assignment.
    a. He will teach you how to fulfill your call as one.
    b. One spouse may already be ministering and waiting for the other to "come along."
        1) Instructions may be different now as the Lord trains you as one.
        2) Be sensitive to the Holy Spirit.

D. Maturing Together/Example of the Plant.

1. Roots of plant must deepen in direct proportion to upward growth [Isaiah 37:31].

2. Your prayer and Word time must increase as you grow in ministry together.
    a. Ministry must flow out of your relationship with God and each other.
    b. As your involvement in your assignment increases, there will be a temptation to decrease your prayer and Word time.
    c. You must discipline yourselves to spend MORE time in these activities.

3. If you outgrow your spiritual root system, your marriage will suffer.

Week 13

Personal Application

Don't be ahead of the Lord.

Special Scriptures

ONE-FLESH MINISTRY

E. Attacks Against One-flesh Ministry.

1. Enemy will send distractions.
   a. We must overcome them.
   b. Proverbs 12:24 (NIV).
      1) Diligence brings rule in area of assignment.
      2) Laziness brings captivity to the desires of the enemy.
   c. Proverbs 22:29 (NIV).
      1) You are called to rule and reign with Jesus.
      2) Become diligent by being schooled by the Holy Spirit.

2. Being secure in your assignment and instructions will prevent enemy from deterring you.
   a. Be single-minded.
   b. Don't allow the enemy to separate you from one another.
      1) This will be his constant goal.
      2) You are wise as serpents and gentle as doves [Matthew 10:16].

F. Evaluation.

1. It is good to periodically stop and evaluate where your one-flesh team is headed.
   a. Need to set Spirit-led goals.
   b. Seek God for His direction in your marriage.
      1) What is your assignment?
      2) What is your next step?
      3) What does God have for you as a couple?
   c. Take time **this week** to fill out the evaluation sheet on page 201.
      1) Bring this sheet with you next week to turn in to your leaders.
      2) This week's homework will provide you with a similar evaluation which you may keep for yourselves.

2. God has a one-flesh assignment for you.
   a. Marriage Ministries International offers opportunity to minister to marriages.
   b. On page 198 of your manual you will find a description of ministry opportunities and requirements.
   c. God bless you both as you continue on from this point with Him.

Personal Application

One flesh ministry - critical to marriage
 danger in going R↗

Special Scriptures

DESTINY IN PROGRESS

Praying for each other:

1. **Couple** _____

   Assignment _____

2. **Couple** _____

   Assignment _____

3. **Couple** _____

   Assignment _____

4. **Couple** _____

   Assignment _____

5. **Couple** _____

   Assignment _____

6. **Couple** _____

   Assignment _____

NOTES

Week 14

Personal Application

Special Scriptures

NOTES

LIFE APPLICATION

WE DO NOT LEARN BY HEARING ONLY, WE ALSO LEARN BY DOING. THAT IS THE PURPOSE OF THIS LIFE APPLICATION MATERIAL.

This Life Application material is designed to further your understanding of the lessons and to enable you as a couple to incorporate the teachings into your daily life. Do all the exercises together each week and space them out over the entire week. Do not wait until the last minute to attempt to complete all the material or you will miss the blessing of God gently integrating His Word continually into your lives.

Each Life Application lesson enables you to delve deeply into the material or to merely skim the surface if you prefer. You will receive as much from the exercise as you are willing to put into it. You set the pace and receive as you choose.

Remember—work **together** on all materials and enjoy this time together. If you are honest with God and with each other, you will be blessed beyond your expectations.

LIFE APPLICATION   WEEK 1 - COVENANT

1. Describe in your own words what covenant relationship means to the two of you.

   When someone promises to do something without expectation of something in return. It is an unconditional guarantee.

2. What were the words of your covenant agreement on your wedding day?

LIFE APPLICATION/WEEK 1 - COVENANT

3. According to what you spoke, what are the promises of your marriage covenant?

What are the terms?

We promised to love and care for one another until one of us dies.

Did you vow before God?

Yes. We spoke our marriage vows before God.

"Whatever your lips utter you must be sure to do, because you made your vow freely to the Lord your God with your own mouth" [Deuteronomy 23:23].

LIFE APPLICATION/WEEK 1 - COVENANT

1) THE COVENANT IN EDEN

God made His first God-man covenant in the Garden of Eden with Adam and Eve. When Adam and Eve fell into sin that Edenic covenant was broken. God, however, immediately set into motion a series of covenants, seven more in all, geared to bring about the redemption of man back into relationship with Him. The connecting thread that runs throughout them demonstrates the faithfulness and undying love of our covenant-keeping God. In order to fully understand our covenant relationship with our Lord and our marriage covenant with each other, we need to briefly follow the covenant line through the Bible.

2) THE COVENANT WITH ADAM

Read Genesis 3:15.

Who is "the seed" of the woman? _____

Who is the word "you" referring to? _____

Look up the word "enmity" in the dictionary. _____

_____

What promise did God make as His part of the covenant?

3) THE COVENANT WITH NOAH

Read Genesis 6:5-9.

One man found favor with God to continue the line of planned salvation for mankind. When He destroyed all life upon the earth, God spared Noah and his family and made a covenant with them.

Read Genesis 9:11-17.

What promise did God make to mankind in this covenant?

no floods
man not cut off from God, destroyed
"rainbow reminder"

LIFE APPLICATION/WEEK 1 - COVENANT

4) THE COVENANT WITH ABRAHAM

Read Genesis 15:4-18.

God now chose a specific group of people through which the Redeemer of man would come. Everything God possessed became available to Abraham when the covenant was cut and everything that Abraham possessed become available to God.

What promise did God make when He cut this covenant?

Genesis 15:5

decendants as many as stars in heavens

Genesis 15:18

land, from river Egypt to Euphrates

Genesis 17:7

line of kings, many nations

What was the sign (seal) of the covenant? [Chapter 17:10]

circumsion

In Genesis 22:2, God demanded something of Abraham as His covenant partner. What was it?

trust + obedience

In covenant relationship, when one partner demands something of the other, the one demanding must be willing to give the same thing in return. When God demanded Abraham's only son, He was free by covenant agreement to sacrifice

his life for Abraham + his decedents
(fill in the blank)

© Marriage Ministries International

LIFE APPLICATION / WEEK 1 - COVENANT

5) THE COVENANT WITH MOSES

Read Exodus 19:5,6.

There is much to the Mosaic covenant, but for now we will concentrate on the giving of the law to the Jewish people. In Exodus 20 the Ten Commandments were given to Moses on the stone tablets. Throughout the books of Exodus, Leviticus, and Numbers more and more laws were given. The law provided a temporary covering for sin so that the Israelites could approach God, but only served to show that none could be made clean (righteous) by observing the law. Read Romans 7:7-25. This passage makes it clear that the Mosaic Law only made man's need for a Savior more evident.

This covenant and the one to follow were covenants with numerous terms which were extremely important to observe.

6) THE COVENANT IN THE WILDERNESS

Read Deuteronomy 8.

Again, when man failed to keep covenant with God, He made yet another covenant in His relentless desire to restore mankind. The first generation of Jews wandering in the desert had failed to keep both the Abrahamic and the Mosaic covenants, so God gave a new covenant to the second generation. This covenant pertained to their possession of the Promised Land and contains the word "land" approximately 180 times. It reaffirmed and amplified the previous covenants. It was clearly a covenant delineating conditions for daily living.

The key word in the terms of this covenant was ___*obedience*___
[Read Deuteronomy 8:20; 11:13; 28:1,2; 28:15 and 30:8.]

7) THE COVENANT WITH DAVID

Read 2 Samuel 7:11-16 and 1 Chronicles 17:10-14.

Now that God had provided and protected the plan for the redemption of man throughout history, He laid the final foundation for Jesus' coming in His covenant with David.

What does God promise in 2 Samuel 7:13? ___*establish earthly throne*___

What does God promise in 2 Samuel 7:16? _____

Through this covenant the throne and kingdom of David were established, pointing ultimately to the eternal kingdom and throne of David's seed. Revelation 3:7 reveals the fulfillment of the Davidic covenant to be _____

8) THE NEW COVENANT

Read Romans 5:12-14 and 1 Corinthians 15:45-49.

Jesus was sent by the Father totally sinless and sharing the same unity (as a man) with the Father that Adam had experienced before he sinned. By maintaining those qualities and never falling into sin, Jesus remained the perfect sacrifice for the redemption of mankind. The new covenant became the *fulfillment* of all the previous covenants.

Read John 3:36. When Adam fell, all men were excluded from an eternal relationship with God. Jesus paid the price for that reunion to take place, and there is no way we can be in relationship with God the Father apart from receiving Jesus personally. God does not recognize religious traditions or honor membership in a certain church or group as a ticket to heaven. Read what Jesus said to people who thought they had it made in Matthew 15:3-6. Jesus requires a personal relationship with each one of us as an entrance into His kingdom. Spiritual death came upon mankind when Adam and Eve sinned in the Garden. A spiritually dead person cannot enter into the kingdom of the living God. A spiritually dead person can have no fellowship with God. There is no way that we can earn our way into a relationship with Him. There is no religious ritual that can cleanse us of our sins. Jesus paid the price for our entrance into God's kingdom—His blood is the only thing that can wash sin away. It is only through receiving Him personally as Lord and Savior that our spirits can come alive. Initially we were born physically. When we receive Jesus, our spirit is reborn, thus, we are born again. Jesus explained it clearly in John 3.

Since covenant relationship is reserved for those who have a personal relationship with the living God, had either one or both of you entered into a personal relationship with Jesus before you were married?

Describe your experience of receiving Jesus as Lord and Savior.

LIFE APPLICATION/WEEK 1 - COVENANT

If this occurred after the marriage had taken place, God was given access to your marriage at that point. If this was your case, when did this occur in your marriage?

Perhaps you cannot remember a specific time that you asked Jesus to be Lord of your life. Or perhaps you have gone to church all your life and have known about Jesus, but do not know Him personally. He is real! He wants a personal relationship with you. If you would like to make that a reality today, say the following prayer out loud to Him. Romans 10:9 says, *"If you confess with your mouth, 'Jesus is Lord', and believe in your heart that God raised Him from the dead, you will be saved."*

****

Jesus, I recognize that there is no way that I can earn forgiveness for my sins. I receive what You did for me on the cross of Calvary. I ask You to forgive all my sins and I receive You as my Lord and my Savior today. Take over my life, Lord, and I will follow You as You lead. I renounce my old way of life and any sinful hold it had on me. I love You, Jesus, and I believe that I am now legally a member of Your family and a resident in Your kingdom. Jesus, You are my Lord!

****

If you have prayed this prayer, you are now born again. Your spirit has come to life in Jesus and every covenant promise is now yours. As a final step to seal this agreement before God and man, sign your name below and put today's date. If doubt ever surfaces again, look back to this date and remember it is accomplished.

_____

_____

_____
DATE

LIFE APPLICATION — WEEK 2 - ONE-FLESH

(Don't forget to cover this material together and to space it out over the entire week.)

Since the original one-flesh couple, Adam and Eve, is to be our model for our one-flesh relationship, let's become as familiar with them and their life as possible. We need to know God's original plan for our one-flesh and how our marriage today compares with that plan.

1. Read Genesis 2:9-10. Can you picture the Garden of Eden? Describe it in your own words.

I picture the Garden of Eden to be like the Amazon basin, not extreme climate and green all the time.

2. Genesis 2:8 gives us a picture of God and man alone in the garden. Adam and Eve were in the center of God's perfect will and were constantly aware of His presence. This is God's will for our homes, too. Can you list some things in your life right now that might keep this from being true in your home?

A. *TV*
B. *Phone*
C. *Activities*
D. *Work schedule*

3. Adam was assigned work in the Garden [Genesis 2:15]. What was he to do?

Adam was to tend and keep the garden.

According to Genesis 1:29, of what did the first couple's diet consist?

fruit and grain

Read Isaiah 1:19 and 2 Thessalonians 3:10. How did Adam's work relate to the livelihood of his household?

Adam's work allowed him good food from the garden. (direct)

LIFE APPLICATION / WEEK 2 - ONE-FLESH

In your home, how does the amount of time spent in work outside the home affect the level of peace within the home? How much work is necessary for provision? How can too much or too little work affect the home?

The more, time spent in work outside the home unbalanced the, the less peace that we have in our home. Not sure. To much work or too little work can cause problems.

4. In Genesis 2:18, God verbalized that Adam needed human companionship and fulfillment so He made him a help "meet" or "suitable, adapted, completing" for him. 1 Peter 3:1, also in the Amplified, instructs wives to adapt themselves to their husbands. What does adapt mean to you?

This means to be, what your husband needs + give to your husband to be successful in the Lord's eyes.

Men need to be admired [Ephesians 5:33 Amplified], encouraged, and respected. If this is not your heart attitude toward your husband, give God permission right now to begin changing it.

5. In Genesis 2:22, God presented Eve to Adam and Adam was excited! Verse 23 records his reaction. God then stated that the attraction to each other would be strong enough for man to leave even the closest relationship that he would know on earth before marriage, his father and mother. Adam recognized and appreciated the wonder and beauty of Eve and knew her importance in his life. 1 Peter 3:7 instructs husbands to live with their wives according to knowledge, honoring them. What does that mean to you?

Treat my wife the way Christ treated the Church, and appreciate my wife, and tell her how special she is.

Women need to be appreciated and loved [Ephesians 5:25]. If this is not your heart toward your wife today, give God permission right now to begin changing it.

LIFE APPLICATION/WEEK 2 - ONE-FLESH

6. Genesis 2:25 tells us that both Adam and Eve were naked and that they were not ashamed. As was discussed in the lesson, the word "both" here indicates equality before God. There is no superior or inferior gender in God's eyes, only different role assignments. Adam and Eve were not ashamed before each other or God. They were able to be totally open with each other and God. There was no area of their life that God was not a part of. Is this characteristic of your marriage today?

Is better and more often the case, but somedays we know we haven't ask God for his guidance.

If not, would you like it to be? Give God permission to begin making those changes today.

7. Genesis 1:28 shows us God's instructions to Adam and Eve for their home and surrounding area. Adam and Eve were told to subdue and rule over the rest of the earth. It is clear that they were not to passively let the rest of the world encroach upon them, but they were to actively affect it. The world today is constantly trying to influence and dominate our homes. Can you name just a few areas of your home life where you have seen this to be true?

TV - media
Politics - certain movements (Gay - Homosexual Agenda)

How can you effectively "subdue and dominate" in those areas?

Turn it off and vote for moral, God fearing candidates.

8. Adam and Eve had total unity and harmony of spirit, soul, and body. Their relationship with each other and with God was perfection, truly made in heaven. Satan recognized the power of that unity and desired to create strife and separation from God. He influenced man and woman to fulfill self instead of their one-flesh relationship. First one spouse disobeyed, then the other one followed. The disobedience of one spouse never justifies the disobedience of the other. Satan only succeeds in separating us more and more when we take that attitude. What are some areas where you have said, "Well, if he/she is going to do that, then I'm going to do this"?

When we are upset with one another, spending, and tempermant.

Begin increasing your awareness of the enemy's subtle attacks. His one goal is to create disunity and cause you to function as two instead of one. At first, what he presents is usually appealing and seemingly very good. As the Lord increases your knowledge regarding the power and unity of your one-flesh relationship, you are going to be fine-tuning your "early warning" systems so that you will be able to pick up on the enemy's attempts long before he succeeds in separating you through strife.

© Marriage Ministries International

LIFE APPLICATION/WEEK 2 - ONE-FLESH

9. When God established marriage, it was His plan that only death could break the covenant relationship. If you have been divorced and are now remarried, perhaps this lesson gave you new insight into God's covenant plan. If you have not already done so, it is important that you repent of both the divorce and the remarriage, since neither was God's plan for your life. Repentance breaks the cycle of condemnation that justification of sin produces. It sets you free to receive the fullness of God's blessing for your present marriage, establishing in your heart that marriage covenant is for life. If this is your desire now, please pray this prayer.

<u>Spouse who was previously married</u>

"Father, I recognize that divorce is not Your solution to marital problems and that I was not in Your will when I divorced. I repent of the sin of divorce and receive Your full forgiveness and pardon. Never again will I allow the enemy to condemn me for my sin.

I recognize that remarriage was also against Your Word and Your will for me, and I repent of committing adultery when I remarried. I receive Your full forgiveness and will never again allow the enemy to speak to me of this matter."

<u>Spouses Together</u>

Because remarriage is adultery according to the Word of God, as spouses you need to repent to each other and receive each other's forgiveness for beginning your marriage on those grounds.

"I ask you (name of spouse) to forgive me also for causing you to commit adultery by marrying me."

After you have forgiven each other, pray this prayer together.

"Father, we thank you for Your forgiveness and that Your mercies are new every morning. Today we establish our marriage covenant upon the Lordship of Jesus Christ. We establish our relationship on a new, firm foundation in Him and promise to be faithful to each other until death separates us. We refuse old patterns and old excuses and from this day forth our testimony will be faithful to Your Word."

Date 3/6/05   Signed _(signature)_

Date March 6, 2005   Signed Lisa Agnes

LIFE APPLICATION   WEEK 3 - ROLES

This lesson is designed to clarify the dual responsibility of husband and wife in marriage. **It does not concentrate on headship and submission**. It may, however, have changed the way you have perceived headship and submission in the past.

1. In light of this teaching, what is your understanding of headship?

    Headship in the final front or ultimate responsibility.

    Is this different than what you believed it to be before?

    No/Yes

    If so, how?

    It became more clear. The headship is not a dictatorship but a partnership with the ultimate responsibility.

    What scripture(s) best depict(s) for you how Jesus functioned in headship?

    Spiritual Headship - taught disciples how to pray

Life Application / Week 3 - Roles

Again—this lesson is designed to clarify the dual responsibility of husband and wife.

2. In light of this teaching, what is your understanding of submission?

Submission is yielding your will to a higher authority. You still have imput but we all answer to a higher authority.

Is this different than what you believed it to be before?

Yes.

If so, how?

That submit is not one person always getting their way.

What scripture(s) best depict(s) for you how the church functions in submission to Jesus?

3. God has created us as man and woman to complete and balance each other. When we are flowing as the Holy Spirit directs us, we will always complement the actions of our spouse. We will flow differently at different times and according to our personalities, but if it is directed by God, it will always be in balance. The following graph illustrates this dynamic. Let us use as an example "listening". It stands to reason that if one spouse is talking, the other should be listening. The amount each spouse spends in listening will depend on how much the other one is talking.

▬▬▬▬ = Husband   ▭▭▭▭ = Wife

This is an average of the husband listening 50 percent of the time and the wife listening 50 percent of the time.

At any given time, though, the amount of time each one is listening to the other may vary accordingly:

If we are moving as the Spirit leads us, we will constantly be flowing along this continuum, back and forth and complementing each other. As we graph what one spouse is doing, the corresponding action on the part of the other spouse should flow in a corresponding fashion.

Listening:

Sharing:

When one is sharing, the other is listening. The amount of listening on the part of one spouse balances the amount of sharing on the part of the other spouse.

When we look closely at how we flow in various areas, we begin to identify patterns in our relationship of husband and wife that we might not otherwise notice. Some of these patterns are godly and are directed of the Spirit. Other patterns are ungodly and are directed by self.

Graph the following areas as the two of you flow most of the time. The width of the graph may even vary according to the total amount of that particular activity that you both accomplish together. For instance, if your sex life is dead, the category of INITIATING LOVE-MAKING may contain very little activity on either part. However, if MIN-

LIFE APPLICATION/WEEK 3 - ROLES

ISTERING TO EACH OTHER is something that you do a great deal, then that graph will be very wide probably covering the full width provided.

Example: ▇▇▇ = Husband   ☐ = Wife

Listening
[■■■■■ | ░░░░░░░░░░]

Listening
[   ]

Disciplining Children
[   ]

Ministering Outside the Home
[   ]

Encouraging
[   ]

Ministering to Each Other
[   ]

Spending Time in the Bible
[   ]

Initiating Love-Making
[   ]

Socializing
[   ]

© Marriage Ministries International

LIFE APPLICATION/WEEK 3 - ROLES

4. There are some areas of our relationship in which the Lord has given us characteristics that He intended to flow together to create a balance. An example of this is "compassion" and "objectivity." As a rule, one spouse is usually more compassionate and sees things from a "soft-hearted" point of view. The other spouse is usually more objective and sees things from a practical and expedient point of view. When these two attributes flow in balance, circumstances will be dealt with as the Lord would have them, firmly and with compassionate understanding. If these areas are out of balance, however, circumstances will tend to be handled with either uncontrollable emotion or hard-hearted coldness.

Jesus was perfectly balanced in His ministry and His desire is for us to move in balanced unity with each other in our one-flesh relationship. Consider some areas where the two of you have trouble achieving this balance. They are usually our areas of greatest friction. It may be "saving" vs. "spending" or "productivity" vs. "leisure." In any given area if we permit our own personal desires to take over, we usually end up in strife. If we allow the Holy Spirit to direct us in complementing each other, however, we blend beautifully in just the right balance.

What are your areas of seeming conflict? On the following form each of you, in your own words, write what you consider your position or viewpoint for each area of concern. You may use the Areas of Concern provided or cross them out and write your own. Do not judge each other's position; only state your own. If each of you writes as you see it, it will be a positive attribute. Remember, do not judge the other's statement; only record your own.

Area of Concern	Husband's Position	Wife's Position
Example Rearing Children	Discipline + Respect / Set Clear Limits	Show by example / Give Room to Develop
Finances	Spend to much	Discipline S+S
In-laws		
Making Love	More Importance	Don't forget us
Nutrition and exercise	More Exercise + Healthier	Improve + make time
Church Attendance	Important	min Weekly
Charitable Giving	more better	Above tithe
Home Maintenance	No time for	Higher Priority

Now look at the words your spouse used to describe his/her position. It should describe a very positive character quality. Very often when we feel strongly about something in an area, it is because we consider what we prefer to do as a very positive action. This would probably not be a problem, if we were operating alone. However, once we enter into the covenant of marriage, we are no longer independent. Very often God uses qualities in each of us to blend together into a balance. They are usually qualities that we feel very strongly about and do not wish to have altered. Because we feel

© Marriage Ministries International

strongly about our own position, we usually feel our spouse's position is wrong. God wants us to begin to release our own opinions to learn to blend together into His one-flesh plan for us.

5. Here's how God brings us into one-flesh balance in these areas. Remember the bar graph that was used to describe how we flow in our relationship? Let us expand our understanding of the dynamics of that flow.

The above diagram represents a closed-loop system. In this system the power source is at the upper portion of the diagram and the recipients of the power are in the lower position.

In a closed-loop system, power flows from the power source down both pathways to the recipients and moves the recipients back and forth depending upon which one is receiving more power at a given time.

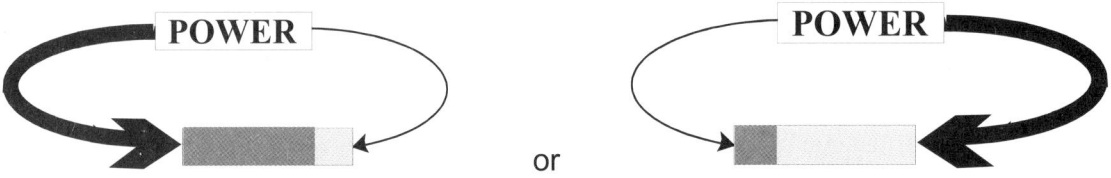

In this type of system, if either one of the recipients does not respond to the power flowing to it, tremendous pressure is created on the other recipient.

So what does all this have to do with husbands and wives? Let's look at this same diagram with God as the power source and husband and wife being the two recipients of the power.

LIFE APPLICATION/WEEK 3 - ROLES

Using this same concept, power (anointing) flows from God (the power source) to each of the recipients (husband and wife), with the amount of power flowing to each one varying from time to time. The diagrams below represent situations in which more power is flowing toward first the husband and then the wife.

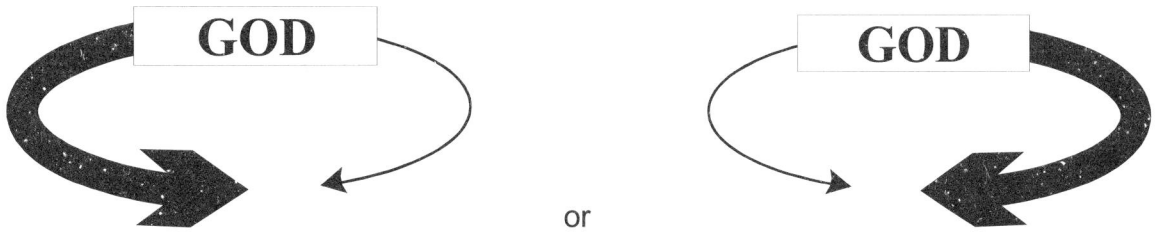

Remember that we said that responsibility is merely responding to ability that God has placed within us? This is how God enables us to respond. He pours out His power and anointing in areas where He gives the responsibility. As long as each spouse responds to the anointing of God, we will flow smoothly back and forth in varying degrees of activity.

When the power is coming from the power source (God) the pressure will flow as God directs. If both partners are sensitive to the Holy Spirit, the dynamics of the flow will continue back and forth as He directs.

If we move in the flesh, however, the pressure then comes from one of us and the dynamics of the flow change drastically. Just as in the example of the closed loop system, lack of response to the power source will apply great pressure to the other recipient.

Say, for instance, that a wife wishes her husband would minister more. If the wife decides in the flesh that the way to make her husband minister more is for her to refuse to minister, it could be illustrated with the following diagram.

© Marriage Ministries International

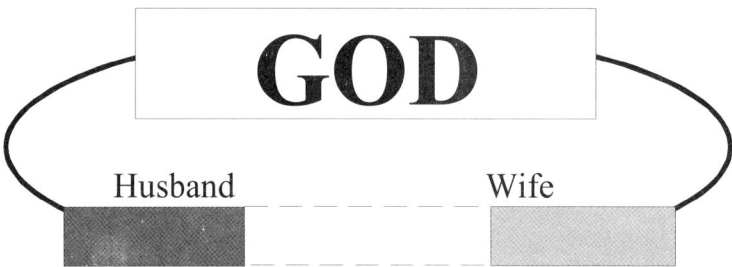

As she draws back, she creates a gap in the continuous flow of their interaction. The resulting effect brings tremendous pressure on her husband. Instead of causing him to minister more, the pressure actually drives him in the opposite direction. We could diagram the effect like this:

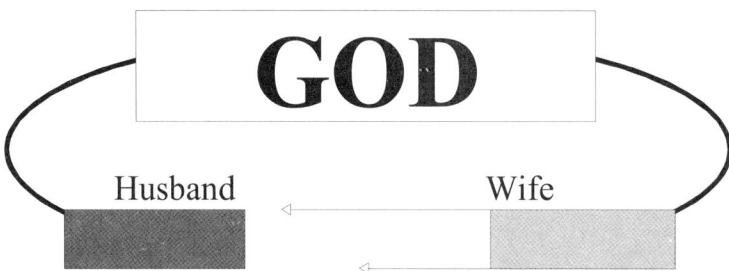

Anytime we place demands on each other to change, the resulting pressure creates just the opposite of what we wish to achieve. Doing things in the flesh will never solve a problem. The only way to bring the power for change into our spouse's life is through intercessory prayer on his/her behalf. Keep to the standard of "Pray it on them; don't lay it on them." The pressure for change then comes from God Who also supplies the power for that change. Both the power and the pressure then flow from above and the dynamic flow between husband and wife remains stable.

We must be sensitive to the Spirit of God as He directs us to move to a greater or lesser degree in any area. If that area is clearly scripturally assigned to one specific partner, then we automatically know who is to flow predominantly in that area. If one spouse is out of order in how he or she is flowing, it is not corrected by the other spouse flowing out of God's will. If you feel that your spouse is not flowing as God would have him or her, remember to take that to the Lord in prayer. Do not attempt to rush in to fill the gap. If the Lord has not called you to that responsibility, you will not be supplied with the power required to carry it out. Too many Christian families are out of order today because each spouse is attempting to fulfill the other's position and not praying for their spouse in those areas of lack. Remember, **pray it on them; don't lay it on them.**

LIFE APPLICATION   WEEK 4 - SOWING AND REAPING

Whether we realize it or not, we have been sowing and reaping all our married life. During this life application we are going to examine the crops we have produced, and decide which ones we want to perpetuate and which ones we want to destroy. Once we have dealt with the old crops, we will begin sowing new ones.

1. Begin to look at each aspect of your family as a gardening area. Become aware of what has been sown and what crops have been produced. There is sometimes a tendency to concentrate on what is wrong. Remember to look for good crops, also. In each of the following areas examine what you have reaped and then determine what you have sown to produce that crop. First look at the harvest and then figure out what seed was sown to produce that crop. Record the harvest in each garden and the seeds sown on each seed bag.

EXAMPLE

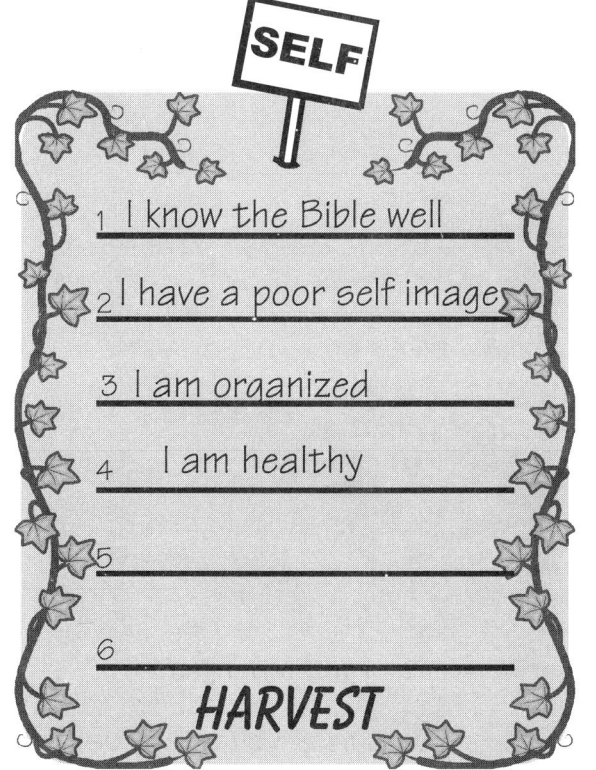

SELF — HARVEST
1. I know the Bible well
2. I have a poor self image
3. I am organized
4. I am healthy
5.
6.

SELF — SEEDS
1. I read my Bible daily
2. I criticize myself a lot
3. I take time to plan
4. I eat wisely and exercise
5.
6.

© Marriage Ministries International

LIFE APPLICATION/WEEK 4 — SOWING AND REAPING

WHAT WAS REAPED

HUSBAND

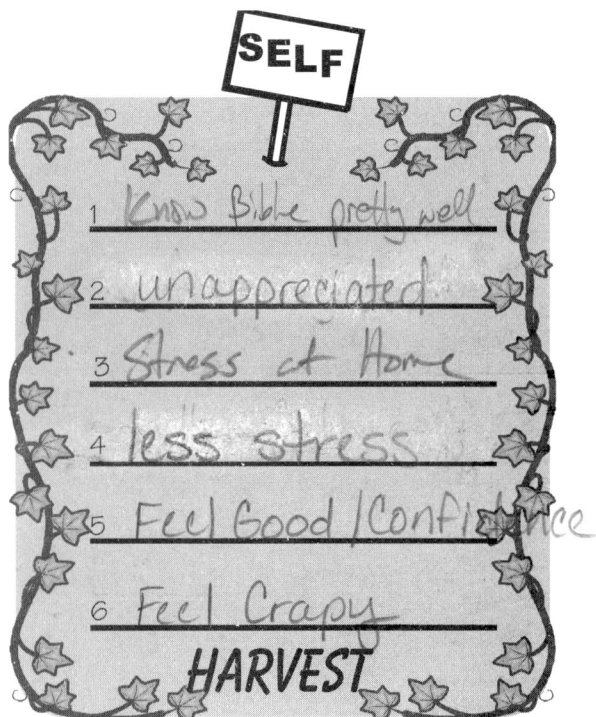

HARVEST:
1. Know Bible pretty well
2. unappreciated
3. Stress at Home
4. less stress
5. Feel Good / Confidence
6. Feel Crapy

WHAT WAS SOWN

SELF

SEEDS:
* 1. Listen / Read
2. No time for self
3. Work too much
* 4. planning
* 5. Look Good
6. Lack of Excercise

WIFE

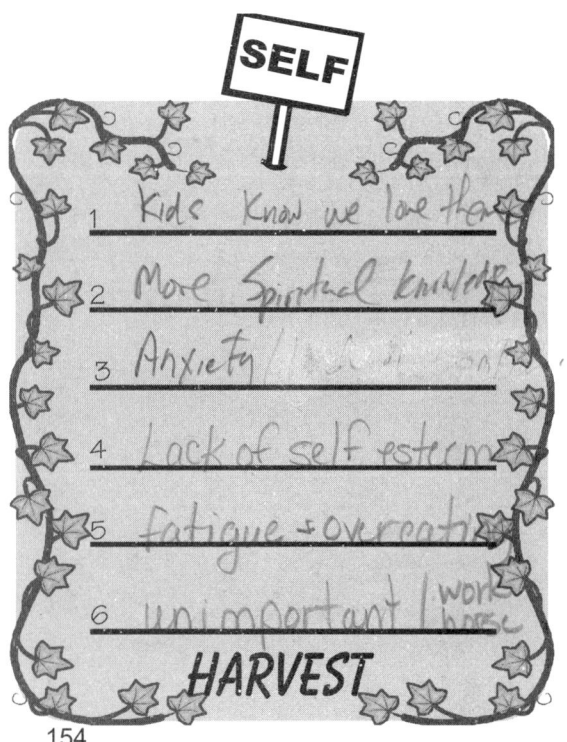

HARVEST:
1. Kids know we love them
2. More Spiritual knowledge
3. Anxiety
4. Lack of self esteem
5. fatigue + overeating
6. unimportant / work horse

SELF

SEEDS:
* 1. open / loving
* 2. Home Schooling
3. yelling
4. critizing
5. lack of healthy eating
6. putting everything for me last

© Marriage Ministries International

LIFE APPLICATION/WEEK 4 – SOWING AND REAPING

SPOUSE (WHAT HUSBAND HAS SOWN IN WIFE)

HARVEST (sign: SPOUSE)
lack of trust
1. communication shut down
2. biblical conversations
3. more responsive
4. feel like saying s— lazy
5. don't care about our home
6. TEAM - score

SEEDS (SPOUSE bag)
1. demean / talk to way
2. listen + reading + discussion *
3. talk / listening
4. complain
5. unwilling to do projection
6. make plans / follow thru * for family

SPOUSE (WHAT WIFE HAS SOWN IN HUSBAND)

HARVEST (sign: SPOUSE)
1. stress / low self esteem
2. trust
3. loved
4. became the same
5. valued
6. devalued / unimportant

7. Peace + contentment

SEEDS (SPOUSE bag)
1. demanding
2. understanding work *
3. patience *
4. yelling
5. make time for him #1 *
6. put him behind everything

7. House clean

© Marriage Ministries International

CHILDREN (WHAT WE EACH HAVE SOWN IN OUR CHILDREN)

HARVEST:
1. Anxiety/Lack of Confidence
2. Proud of their behavior
3. better spiritual knowledge
4. no memories
5. giving/compassionate
6. responsibility

SEEDS:
1. Yelling/Criticize
2. discipline correctly
3. home schooling
4. not enough family act.
5. serve others
6. Chores

HOME (WHAT WE EACH HAVE SOWN INTO OUR HOME)

HARVEST:
1. better organized
2. feel bad about house + us
3.
4.
5.
6.

SEEDS:
1. throw out junk
2. don't improve home
3.
4.
5.
6.

LIFE APPLICATION/WEEK 4 — SOWING AND REAPING

2. Now examine the harvests you have reaped. Are there good harvests you want to see continued? Star (*) those seeds which have produced good crops. Continue planting and replanting them.

Are there any weeds? Do you want them to stop growing? If so, repent and spray the weed killer on them. Using a red marking pencil, draw a line through those weeds. The blood of Jesus covers every confessed sin. Those weeds are now dying off. You may continue to see traces of them for a while. Just remember, as long as you don't sow bad seeds, there are not going to be any more weeds. If you do catch yourself sowing any undesirable seeds, repent immediately and they will not come to harvest.

3. Now to plant new crops. First, you must cultivate the soil. If you are sowing into yourself, spend time in prayer and in the Word. If you are sowing into someone else, spend time in intercession and spiritual warfare. Keep the soil well-watered with the Word of God. Here are the directions for planting.

2 Corinthians 9:10 tells us, *"Now He who supplies seed to the sower and bread for food will also increase your store of seed and will enlarge the harvest of your righteousness."* Go to the Lord and ask Him for seed. Obtain your new seed from the Word of God, His expressed will for you and your loved ones. Draw from His seed bag.

Leviticus 19:19b tells us not to sow two crops in the same field. The Word of God will never produce a bad crop. If weeds begin to surface in the garden, we know from whose bag they have come. We cannot sow faith in God and faith in Satan (doubt) in the same field. Be encouraged, what you are planting from the Word is going to come to harvest if you don't give up.

Ecclesiastes 11:4 says, *"Whoever watches the wind will not plant; whoever looks at the clouds will not reap."* If we look to circumstances, we will not sow the proper Word in each situation. We must sow into our marriages as the Lord directs us, regardless of past records or seemingly impossible circumstances.

Finally, we must sow consistently and wait patiently for the new crops to mature. Hebrews 10:35,36 NIV tells us, *"So do not throw away your confidence; it will be richly rewarded. You need to persevere so that when you have done the will of God, you will receive what He has promised."*

****

Record in the following areas the new seed that you are planting into yourself, your spouse, your children, and your home. Then keep a record in each of the gardens as you see the harvests appear.

© Marriage Ministries International

Life Application / Week 4 — Sowing and Reaping

HUSBAND

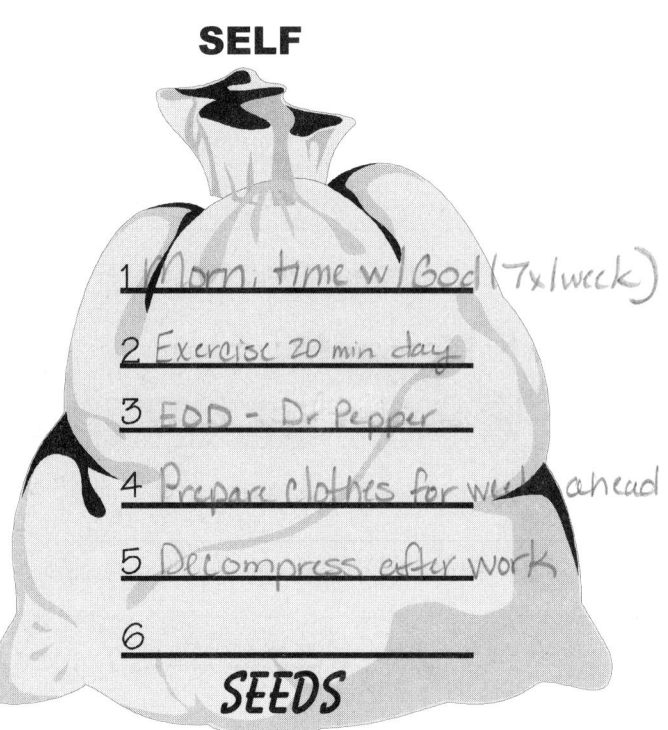

SELF — SEEDS
1. Morn. time w/ God (7x/week)
2. Exercise 20 min day
3. EOD – Dr Pepper
4. Prepare clothes for week ahead
5. Decompress after work
6.

SELF — HARVEST
1.
2.
3.
4.
5.
6.

WIFE

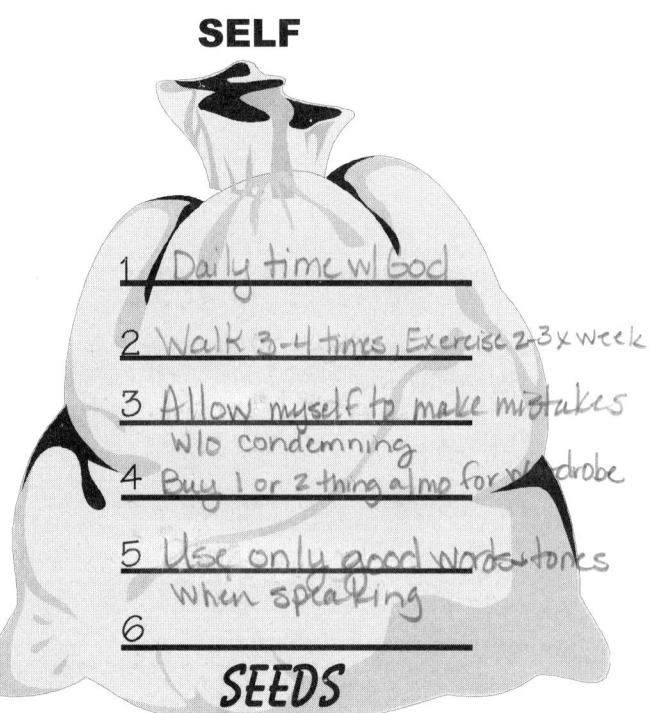

SELF — SEEDS
1. Daily time w/ God
2. Walk 3-4 times, Exercise 2-3x week
3. Allow myself to make mistakes w/o condemning
4. Buy 1 or 2 thing a/mo for wardrobe
5. Use only good words + tones when speaking
6.

SELF — HARVEST
1.
2.
3.
4.
5.
6.

Life Application/Week 4 – Sowing and Reaping

SPOUSE (WHAT HUSBAND IS GOING TO SOW IN WIFE)

SPOUSE — SEEDS:
1. Date wife weekly
2. Pray together @ night
3. Give time for her to relax
4. Clean car weekly
5. Take active interest in home maintenance
6. Flexible w/ kids schedule

SPOUSE — HARVEST:
1.
2.
3.
4.
5.
6.

SPOUSE (WHAT WIFE IS GOING TO SOW IN HUSBAND)

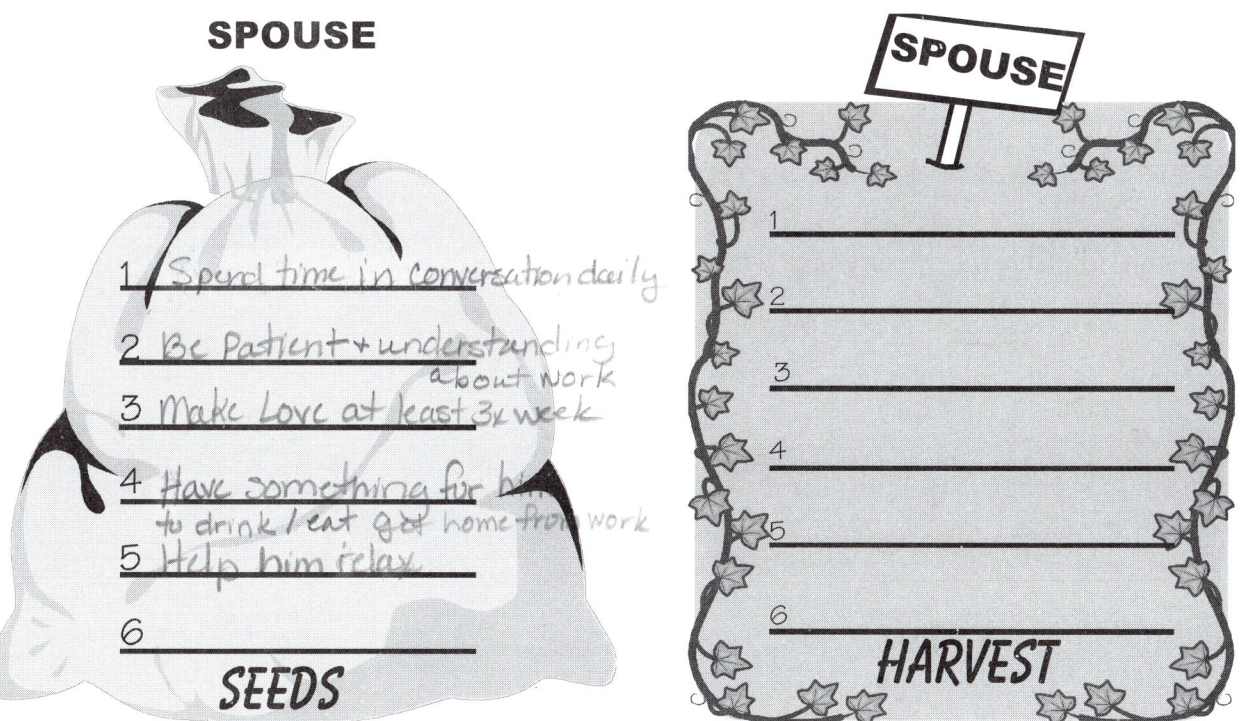

SPOUSE — SEEDS:
1. Spend time in conversation daily
2. Be patient + understanding about work
3. Make love at least 3x week
4. Have something for him to drink/eat get home from work
5. Help him relax
6.

SPOUSE — HARVEST:
1.
2.
3.
4.
5.
6.

© Marriage Ministries International

LIFE APPLICATION/WEEK 4 – SOWING AND REAPING

CHILDREN (WHAT WE ARE EACH GOING TO SOW IN OUR CHILDREN)

CHILDREN — SEEDS
1. Open + Loving
2. Set boundries + follow thru
3. Bed by 9:00 pm — up by 7:00 AM earlier if poss.
4. Prepare healthy meals — 5x week
5. Plan daily activities - even if working
6. Family time (meeting) 1x week
7. 4 trips a year (driving) 3 day weekend
Every 2 yrs vac. w/ family

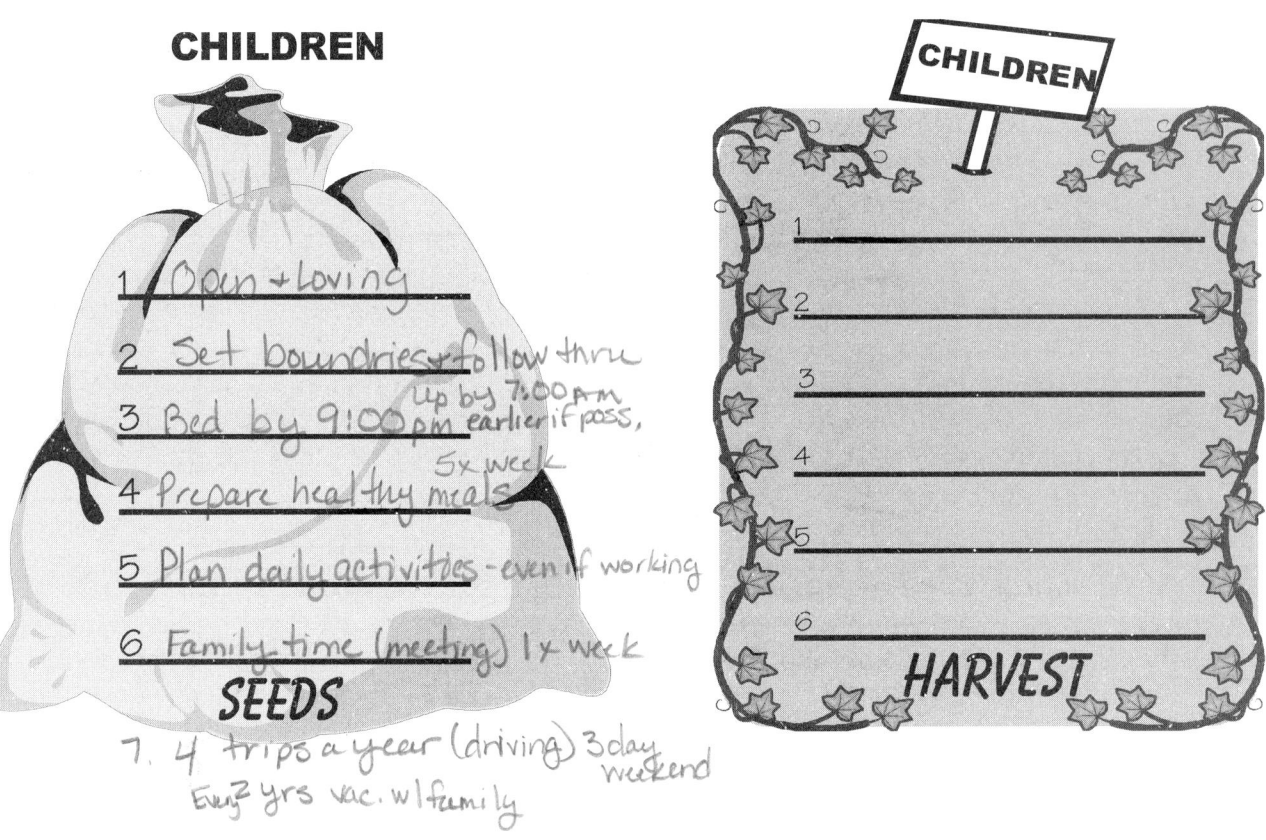

CHILDREN — HARVEST
1.
2.
3.
4.
5.
6.

HOME (WHAT WE ARE EACH GOING TO SOW IN OUR HOME)

HOME — SEEDS
1. Continue to organize 1 item a day
2. Laundry daily (family plan)
3. Do 15-30 min clean up to house as fam.
4. Get lanscape plan - begin some planting
5. School put away daily
6. File away kids paper

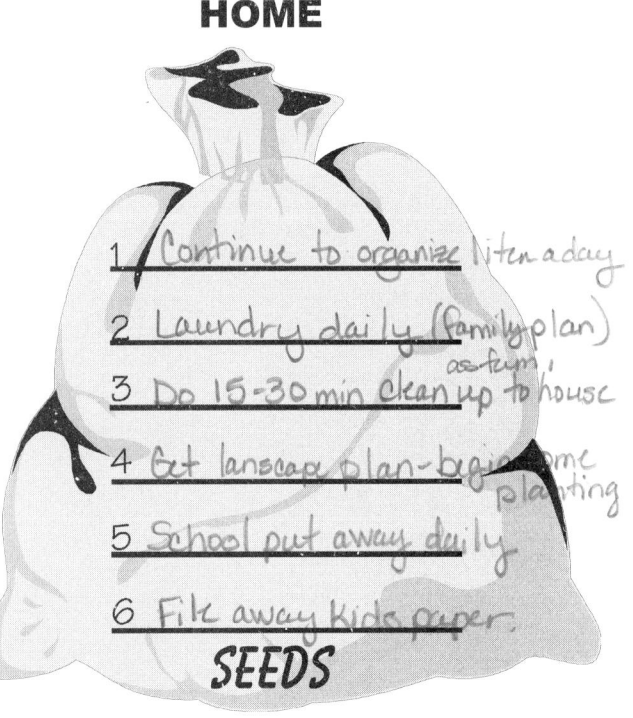

HOME — HARVEST
1.
2.
3.
4.
5.
6.

LIFE APPLICATION/WEEK 4 — SOWING AND REAPING

4. Strife occurs in our lives and in our marriage when we have not been pulling weeds effectively. Satan will give us as many seeds for the sowing as we are willing to receive [Matthew 13:24-27]. As the crops begin to come up, he returns to point them out to us. If he concentrates on the weeds in our own garden, it results in condemnation. If he concentrates on the weeds in our spouse's garden, it results in judgment, criticism, and strife. If we allow the cycle to continue, with the maturation of each new crop of weeds we have new seeds to sow. Satan doesn't play fair. He even brings up old crops that have long since been gone. He will package his seeds in all kinds of attractive wrappers to get us to take them and plant them. The seeds for strife come from these crops of the enemy. We must be quick to recognize these crops as they begin to appear in our gardens. Be diligent—weed your garden every day! If anything begins to appear that is not of God, repent. Matthew 15:13 records Jesus saying, *"Every plant that My heavenly Father has not planted will be pulled up by the roots."* Let this become our standard in caring for our fields.

Do not receive demonic communication regarding your spouse. Examine every thought that you have regarding your spouse and ask yourself, "Would Jesus say that?" If it's not from the Lord, it's from the enemy. There are no neutral seeds. Don't take that death seed and plant it in your garden. Remember, it takes two to engage in strife.

LIFE APPLICATION   WEEK 5 - FORGIVENESS

"And so He condemned sin in sinful man, in order that the righteous requirements of the law might be fully met in us who do not live according to the sinful nature but live according to the Spirit. Those who live according to the sinful nature (flesh) have their minds set on what that nature desires; but those who live in accordance with the Spirit have their minds set on what the Spirit desires. The mind of sinful man is death, but the mind controlled by the Spirit is life and peace because the sinful mind (flesh) is hostile to God. It does not submit to God nor can it do so" [Romans 8:3b-7 NIV].

1. As Christians, it is our goal to be led of the Spirit and not operate in the flesh. Forgiveness is always the leading of the Holy Spirit. God is quick to forgive. *"For You, Lord, are good, and ready to forgive, and abundant in mercy to all those who call upon You."* [Psalm 86:5 NKJV].

List here any reasons that you have used in the past to refuse to forgive.

HUSBAND	WIFE
still mad	not sorry
haven't resolved	haven't asked
don't want to	don't feel like it
	not wrong, justified

Does the Word of God support any of these reasons?

When we hold unforgiveness in our hearts, it is the soul that is wounded. Our soul (mind, will, and emotions) refuses to let go of the hurt and makes a conscious decision to retain the offense. The more we yield to the leading of the Spirit, the more we will be quick to forgive those who have wounded or offended us.

Unforgiveness maintained is very often manifested in the flesh. In 2 Samuel 6, Michal, David's wife, was upset with David for dancing before God in the streets. She held unforgiveness and judgment in her heart and 2 Samuel 6:23 tells us she *"...had no children to the day of her death."* Although we do not usually see such drastic manifestations of unforgiveness, other more common physical ailments can be, but not necessarily are, the direct result of refusing to forgive someone. These can be headaches, ulcers, insomnia, and poor digestion—to name a few.

Why don't you both take time right now to examine your hearts to see if there is anyone toward whom you know you are holding unforgiveness. You need not do this out loud unless you choose to. Be honest with God and with yourself. Do not justify your feelings; just admit they are there.

How about yourself? Do you have trouble forgiving yourself? Many times we feel freer to release others from their guilt than we do to release ourselves. Perhaps it is because we know ourselves all too well, our shortcomings and our failures. A constant feeling of unworthiness is a sure sign that we have unforgiveness toward ourselves. Although we are unworthy, Christ has made us worthy by His blood. Colossians 1:10 and 1 Thessalonians 2:12 both tell us to walk worthy of our calling. There is no way that God could command us to walk worthy if He had not made us so. If God can forgive us, who are we to retain our own sin? Are we more righteous than He? In Genesis 16, Sarai was upset and angry with herself for giving her servant girl to Abram so that she could bear him a child. She took her anger out on Hagar, the servant girl. Hagar despised Sarai and Sarai mistreated Hagar. Often we take our unforgiveness toward self out on others, usually those closest to us or the ones who remind us most of our failure to forgive.

Right now examine your heart and see if there are areas of unforgiveness toward yourself. By an act of your will, choose to forgive yourself. Ask God to help you see yourself as He sees you.

Scripture says that David was a man after God's own heart [Acts 13:22]. Yet we read in the life of David that he committed sin, even murder and adultery. Then how can it be said that he was a man after God's own heart? For one thing, he was quick to forgive. Throughout 2 Samuel we see David again and again offended and wounded, but David was consistent in his forgiveness, keeping his heart pure. When David became involved in adultery with Bathsheba, even arranging for her husband to be killed so that David might have her, he readily admitted his guilt and repented when confronted [2 Samuel 11 and 12]. When the child of that union died despite David's prayer and fasting, he readily forgave himself and did not hold unforgiveness against God. How many of us could have done that, or would we spend years regretting what we had done?

David's son, Absalom, on the other hand, is a classic picture of unforgiveness. In 2 Samuel 13, Amnon raped Absalom's sister. The unforgiveness in Absalom's heart led to murder, conspiracy against the king, envy, strife, and eventually to Absalom's death [2 Samuel 13 to 2 Samuel 18:15]. **We cannot afford** to hold unforgiveness in our hearts. Regardless of what the offense was or how big the failure was, if Jesus could shed His innocent blood for it, we certainly cannot hold an offense against someone else or ourselves. Right now, today, we are going to get rid of that garbage. We are going to free others and ourselves.

2. It is time to let Jesus help you clean house in the area of unforgiveness. First of all, each of you needs to sit down alone and make a list of everyone the Holy Spirit brings to mind that you have not forgiven. He may begin to show you areas of unforgiveness that you have harbored from as far back as childhood. You need to forgive anyone who has ever offended you. This may be a difficult time for you. Some of the feelings of shame, humiliation, and hurt may come flooding back as you remember the offenses. Allow Jesus to heal those hurts as you release forgiveness to each person. (You may wish to speak your forgiveness of them out loud. Sometimes the spoken word has power to "cement" things that have been mere thoughts in your mind.) As you forgive each one, use a red pen to cross them off your list. Let that red ink remind you of the blood of Jesus blotting out each offense. Release to Jesus all who have offended you. Ask Him to help you see each one as He sees them.

LIFE APPLICATION/WEEK 5 - FORGIVENESS

Pray for each other during this time.

(This period that you are alone may take some time. Give each other whatever time is necessary to finish. It may even take several days to work through all of it. Be patient and continue to pray for each other.)

3. When you have each completed your time alone and have forgiven all that the Lord has shown you, come back together. Now ask the Holy Spirit to show you as a couple if there is anyone you have not forgiven that has offended the two of you or your family. As He brings them to mind, forgive them as a one-flesh couple. Pray for each other and encourage each other when forgiving is difficult. Release all hurt and retribution to Jesus. Ask Him to place His compassion for each of the offenders in your hearts.

Consider not only people who have wounded or offended you but also churches, ministries, and organizations. Many people today are carrying unforgiveness toward ministries or previous churches and pastors. Because they have not forgiven them, they cannot settle peacefully in any church or support any ministry. No matter what the offense, you need to forgive and release them to the Lord. Do not let the woundings of the past cripple your relationships today.

If there are those who have offended your entire family and if you sense your children are ready for this, you may wish to gather the whole family together and forgive those who have wounded all of you. If you do not believe your children are ready for this now, you as a couple need to forgive the offenders in the name of your family and pray for the day when the children will also be able to release them in forgiveness.

4. Ask the Lord to show you if either of you have taken up the offense of others. Is there anyone that has wounded your spouse or your children that you are refusing to forgive? Have you sided with friends or relatives in a conflict they have had with someone else? Are you finding it difficult to forgive those who have offended them?

If you realize that you have taken up another person's offense, repent of having done so. Then forgive the offender. If the offended person is your spouse, help him or her to forgive the offender if they have not already done so. Give each other permission to help in the future should either of you take up someone else's offense again. Our spouses can usually see more clearly when we are doing this than we can ourselves. Agree to help each other get healed when wounding occurs.

5. Finally, the time has come for you to forgive each other for any offenses, disappointments, repeated commissions or omissions (things you have done or have failed to do), and anything else that the Holy Spirit shows you. Share this forgiveness with

each other after a time of prayer together. This is not a time to accuse or lay guilt on each other. Treat each other with the mercy and tenderness that you would want of Jesus if you were talking with Him about your own sin.

As you forgive each other, also repent for any times that you have brought up past sins that had already been forgiven. When you are finished with all the Lord has shown you, pray this prayer together:

"Lord, Jesus, today we receive Your forgiveness for our sins. We will not remember them anymore. We receive Your compassion for each other and determine from this day forth to walk in love and mercy toward each other. Wash us now with Your blood. Cleanse us from all unrighteousness. Let our hearts be tender toward each other.

Let Your love cover a multitude of sins. May we see each other through Your eyes from now on. Today we believe we have received this in Your Name. Amen."

6. Now comes the time to walk out the forgiveness you have given and received. If one spouse stumbles, let the other help him or her up [Ecclesiastes 4:10]. Each time, continue to ask yourself, "Am I treating this person the way I want Jesus to treat me when I sin?" A couple that is quick to forgive can overcome any obstacles the devil throws in their path.

Continue to pray for each other. Continue to draw on the power of God, His compassion and His mercy. Keep your eyes on Jesus and the offenses of others will seem small by comparison to His great forgiving love.

LIFE APPLICATION   WEEK 6 - FAITH VISION AND TRUST

This week we are going to seek the Lord for His faith vision for our spouses and for our marriages. On the surface this assignment will seem short, but if you do it thoroughly, you will find it most fulfilling and exciting. **The first two sections should be completed alone by each spouse. The third section should be done together.**

Remember, this is God's vision for your spouse and your marriage, not what you want them to be. Pray and ask Him to give you scriptures that describe your spouse and your marriage as He sees them. Write them down and pray them daily for each other and for your marriage. Allow the Lord to share with you His excitement over what you are praying for each other.

If you are not that familiar with the Word and are not quite sure where to start, there are many "generic" scriptures that speak of God's vision for a godly man and a godly woman. You may wish to use these to get started and then let God begin to fine tune His specific vision for your spouse and marriage.

EXAMPLE: Psalm 1 is a good description of a godly man. A wife whose husband's name is John may write, *"Blessed is John who does not walk in the counsel of the wicked or stand in the way of sinners or sit in the seat of mockers. But John's delight is in the law of the Lord...etc."*

A man whose wife's name is Mary might state from Proverbs 31, *"Mary is worth far more than rubies. I have full confidence in her and I lack nothing of value. She brings me good, not harm, all the days of her life...etc."*

HUSBAND

1. In the following section, write the faith vision you are believing for your wife. Use a concordance or topical index from a study Bible, if necessary, to find scriptures that depict what the Lord desires her to be. (No coaching from the wives. This is his assignment.)

Proverbs 18:22
Proverbs 19:14
Romans 5:3

LIFE APPLICATION/WEEK 6 – FAITH VISION AND TRUST

WIFE

2. In the following section, write the faith vision you are believing for your husband. Use a concordance or a topical index from a study Bible, if necessary, to find scriptures that depict what God desires for him to be. (No coaching from the husbands. This is her assignment.)

Char. trait you see bible verse that lines up with.

Good + upright person in his work + prosper

Proverb 1:5 + 7 knowledge, wisdom begins w/a fear of the Lord

LIFE APPLICATION/WEEK 6 — FAITH VISION AND TRUST

ONE FLESH

3. Now the two of you together, write a vision for your marriage, your life together. Use the Word to describe both short-term and long-term goals.

Nm 31:25-30 268 - portion of war spoils
Dct 25:4 p.315
Nch 13:10 p.827

Act 18:24-28 - Aquila + Priscilla
Joshua 24:15

1 Corinthian 9:24-27 Discipline my body + bring it into subjection,
Practice what you preach

Ezekiel 3:8-9+10 - God makes us strong, God's word must sink into our hearts before we can help others

4. As you stand in faith for the visions the Lord has given you, keep the following steps in mind.

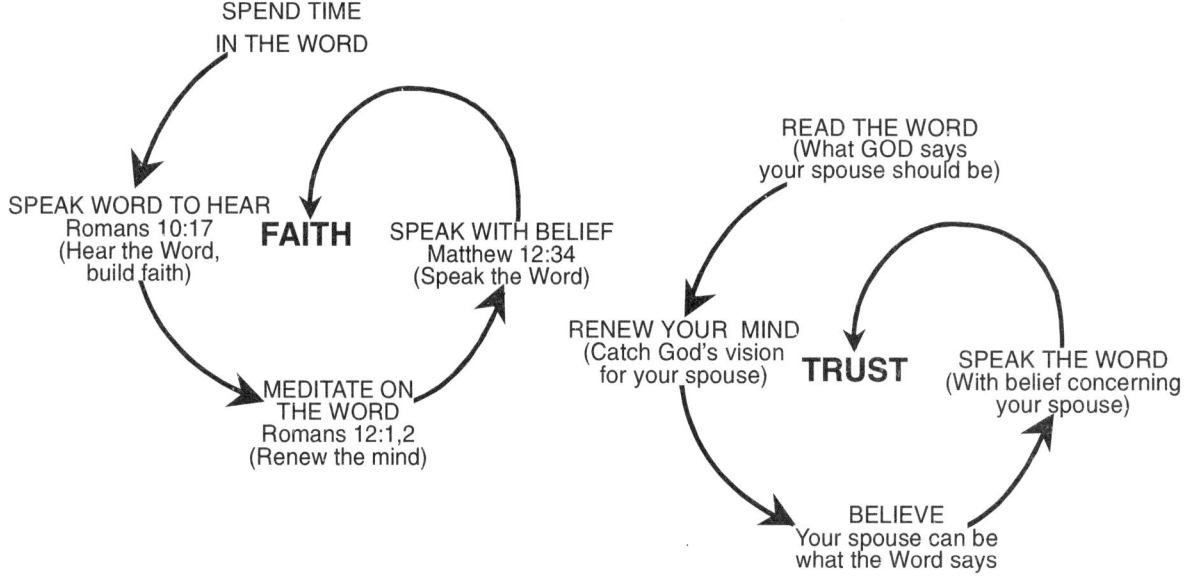

LIFE APPLICATION   WEEK 7 - PRAYING TOGETHER

ine to develop your prayer life together
ie to start. As was shared in the lesson,

it may be like learning to ride a bicycle --
itient with yourselves and allow the Holy
ick a time daily to pray together. At first,
u spend praying, only that you do it to-
about. The enemy knows the power in
rything he can to discourage and delay
itment daily and discipline yourselves to

in the spirit together. This knits you as
ying in your native language, be sure to
ations for which you are praying. If you
are having difficulty getting started, remember it takes more maturity to pray in your native language together, so start by praying in the spirit. Take time during your prayer time together to share with each other what God is saying to you individually. Let this be a special time of communication with God and each other.

If you already have a prayer time together, use this as a time to allow the Lord to deepen and strengthen it.

If you do not already have a prayer journal, you might consider using the following one. There is a section to record what you pray for each day and what the Lord says when He speaks to you. Following that is a section to record scriptures you are praying. There is also a section to record any special instructions or insights that you received while praying - any "new light" shed on those things for which you are praying. Finally, there is a section in which to record the answers you receive to prayer. We have included two pages here. If you like this format, make copies of a page and continue on with it. You may prefer to use another one or make up one of your own -- just use some consistent way to keep a journal of your prayer time together.

© Marriage Ministries International

LIFE APPLICATION/WEEK 7 — PRAYING TOGETHER

DATE 4/10/05

PRAYER TOPICS

Children - James (anger + frustration), Lauren (same) Caroline (listen) Catherine, decision about job, house, finances, discipline in all

WORDS RECEIVED FROM THE LORD

SCRIPTURES PRAYED

Prov 1:4 - To the young man (or girl) knowledge + discretion
Prov 1:8 My son hear the instruction of your father + not foresake the law of your mother

INSTRUCTIONS RECEIVED OR INSIGHT GAINED

Act 18:24-28 - Aquila + Priscilla

ANSWERED PRAYER

LIFE APPLICATION / WEEK 7 — PRAYING TOGETHER

DATE 4/16/05

PRAYER TOPICS

Rest & Refresh, Gene & Kathleen, Gile & Connie, More daily time spent in the word, James (feel our unconditional love), Lauren (anger & self confidence), Caroline (listening & behavior), Catherine (rest & comfort/security)

WORDS RECEIVED FROM THE LORD

Heather - unhappiness → contentment, Mom - health, Byron - ", Moma - hair → stress

SCRIPTURES PRAYED

Proverbs 22:6 Train up a child in the way (he) should go and when he is old he will not depart from it.
Ex 16:23

INSTRUCTIONS RECEIVED OR INSIGHT GAINED

ANSWERED PRAYER

© Marriage Ministries International

LIFE APPLICATION/WEEK 7 — PRAYING TOGETHER

Have you received the Baptism or the Infilling of the Holy Spirit? If not, there's no better time than the present to receive all that God has for you. If you want to be baptized by Jesus in the Holy Spirit, pray the following prayer.

"Lord Jesus, I want all that You have for me. I want to surrender all to You. Please baptize me in the Holy Spirit right now. I receive it. Thank you."

With both of you baptized in the Holy Spirit, you can pray with your understanding in your native language and in the spirit in tongues. Sometimes we don't know how to pray or what we should say. *"In the same way, the Spirit helps us in our weakness. We do not know what we ought to pray, but the Spirit Himself intercedes for us with groans that words cannot express."* [Romans 8:26 NIV]. It is at times such as these that we need to pray in the spirit for He knows how to pray a perfect prayer, always in the will of God. Begin praying both ways in your daily prayer time together. Remember that praying in the spirit also edifies [1 Corinthians 14:4].

If you received the Baptism of the Holy Spirit this week, do the same as you did when you were born again. Write the date below and sign your name. It is established for all eternity!

_____
DATE

_____
HUSBAND

_____
WIFE

LIFE APPLICATION — WEEK 8 - AGREEMENT

1. Identify some way that you as a couple have used to come into agreement in the past.

   over house decisions

   over car decisions

   over school decisions

2. What have been the results of these methods?

   — less than the best
   — some argueing, fighting

LIFE APPLICATION/WEEK 8 - AGREEMENT

3. Consider a matter that you need to come into agreement about right now. What does the Word of God say concerning it?

- James Car
- School for kids next year

If you can't find anything specific concerning it in the Word, begin praying together in the spirit to seek God's will for the situation. Remember that you must lay down all preconceived notions of what the "correct" answer is and pray in the spirit until you have the same answer from the Holy Spirit. This may take several times of prayer before you come to the point of both of you hearing the same thing. Do not become discouraged. It is well worth the time it takes to proceed in the perfect will of God.

SUBJECT WHICH REQUIRES AGREEMENT _____

DATE PRAYER BEGAN _____

FINAL ANSWER RECEIVED BY BOTH HUSBAND AND WIFE IN AGREEMENT

WITH THE LORD _____

_____

DATE FINAL ANSWER RECEIVED _____

RESULTS

_____
_____
_____
_____

When you have reached agreement on the first topic, move on to others. What else do you desire to know God's perfect will concerning? Remember, always seek God's will together. Do not assume that one has heard from God and just "go along

LIFE APPLICATION/WEEK 8 - AGREEMENT

with it." The enemy has no power against your decision-making as a couple when you stand united in agreement with God.

"Though one can be overpowered, two can defend themselves. A cord of three strands is not quickly broken" [Ecclesiastes 4:12 NIV].

SUBJECT	ANSWER

LIFE APPLICATION
Week 9 - Flowing Together in the Spirit

1. From the day we are born-again, the Holy Spirit begins developing the fruit of the Spirit within us. As He works, some character qualities are developed faster than others. Listed below are the nine character qualities which comprise the fruit of the Spirit.

Love—agape, God's unconditional love, not based on feelings.
Joy—deeper than happiness, it is not dependant upon circumstances.
Peace—more than absence of strife, it is security, safety and tranquility.
Patience—endurance, steadfastness.
Kindness—gentleness, integrity.
Goodness—uprightness of heart and life.
Faithfulness—fidelity, one who can be relied upon, covenant keeping.
Gentleness—strength under Godly control.
Self-control—mastery of desires and passions.

In the space below, record which of these character qualities you feel are **the most matured** in your life and give an example of how you saw this demonstrated recently.

HUSBAND

Character Quality	Example
goodness, love, faithfulness	

WIFE

Character Quality	Example
faithfulness, gentleness	When the children are scared or sick

2. Now list the character qualities that you feel are the **least developed** in your life. Scripture tells us, *"Walk in the Spirit, and you shall not fulfill the lust of the flesh. For the flesh lusts against the Spirit, and the Spirit against the flesh; and these are*

contrary to one another, so that you do not do the things that you wish" [Galatians 5:16,17]. Beside each character quality below, list a way in which you can walk in the Spirit and not fulfill the desires of your flesh.

HUSBAND

Character Quality	Way of Walking in the Spirit and Denying My Flesh
thoughts all the rest	
self control	think before I speak — knowing when I try to manipulate situations
peace	need to relax about things more & trust God more

WIFE

Character Quality	Way of Walking in the Spirit and Denying My Flesh
Kindness	watch words - edify the Lord
joy	appreciate family, not worry about sm items
gentleness	consistency

3. Sometimes it is easier for others to see the development of spiritual fruit within us. Take time now to share with your spouse a character quality that you have seen developing within him or her as the Holy Spirit has worked in his or her life.

4. As the Holy Spirit works within each of you, remember that Jesus always challenged the individual heart when there was a relational problem. When conflict arises between the two of you, be open to the Lord's challenge to your own heart. No matter what your spouse is saying or doing, the Holy Spirit desires to develop mature character qualities within **you**. The next time you two experience relational conflict, come back to this page and record what the Lord spoke to each of you.

5. 1 Corinthians 12:7 says, *"...to each one the manifestation of the Spirit is given for the common good"* (NIV). *"To each one"* means all who have received Jesus Christ as their Lord and Savior. No one is left out. Do you know the Holy Spirit desires to use you in the gifts to meet the needs of people around you? Be open to the Holy Spirit working through you in any gift that He chooses. Be obedient to His prompting and keep the need of the person or situation in mind. All too often we focus on self and wonder "how will I look" or "what will they think of me." Just be obedient to the Holy Spirit, Whose desire it is to meet a need and let go of all other concerns. Be open and teachable and willing to be used and the Holy Spirit will do the rest.

Our lives may not seem as spectacular as those we read about in scripture, but if we begin to take closer notice, we may see the gifts of the Spirit operating in our lives more than we had realized. Have either of you moved in the gifts of the Spirit? If so, which ones? What needs were met?

6. The Holy Spirit often desires to use us together as husband and wife operating in the gifts. Very often one spouse will get a witness in his or her spirit when the other spouse is about to move in a gift. Has this ever happened to you? Have you moved in the gifts together?

LIFE APPLICATION/WEEK 9 — FLOWING TOGETHER IN THE SPIRIT

7. Our homes are one of the most important places in which we will observe the gifts in operation. Has anyone in your family been used of the Holy Spirit in a gift in your home? What need was met?

    Lauren - w/ Patrick (basket b-day)
    James
    Carolyn

8. As your prayer time together increases in depth, you will begin to see the flow of the Holy Spirit manifesting more and more. Be eager to flow together in the gifts.

    Beginning this week, record every time you observe a gift in operation in your home, with your friends, at church, or wherever it occurs. Don't become discouraged if you don't see a large number at first; just become aware of them when you do see them.

GIFTS IN OPERATION	WHERE OBSERVED	NEED THAT WAS MET

LIFE APPLICATION WEEK 10 - INTIMACY

> **PLEASE NOTE: THIS LESSON INVOLVES EXAMINING PAST SEXUAL ACTIVITY. DO NOT "DUMP" INFORMATION ON YOUR SPOUSE. BEFORE ANY SIN OF THIS NATURE IS SHARED BETWEEN YOU, YOU NEED TO PRAY AND FAST AND PREPARE SPIRITUALLY. LESSON 12 WILL DEAL WITH HOW TO CONFESS SIN BETWEEN YOU AND TO RECEIVE HEALING.**

1. If your sexual relationship needs healing, you need to follow the instructions given in the lesson. Repent of any unconfessed sexual sins and receive forgiveness from the Lord. Forgive yourself. Break all soul ties connected with the sin. Ask the Lord to help you discern any spirits that may have been assigned because of that sin. Cancel, in the name of Jesus, their assignments over you, your spouse, your children and your children's children down through the generations. If you were wounded sexually as a child or an adult, forgive the one or ones who hurt you. Pray the following prayer:

> "Father, in the name of Jesus, I repent of all sexual sin in which I have been involved. I receive Your forgiveness now, in Jesus' name. I choose to forgive others who have hurt me. I choose to forgive myself. Jesus, I ask you now to cleanse out all the bitterness, all the resentment, all the hurt feelings with Your precious blood. I now break any and all ungodly soul ties with .... (speak out every name God gives you). I break all of the authority connected with these ties in my life and I declare that I am loosed from all affects now, this day. I renounce Satan and all his works from my life. I take authority, in the name of Jesus, over any spirits assigned because of this sin,................(names of spirits the Lord reveals to you). I cancel their assignment over me, over my spouse, over our marriage, over our children, and over our children's children down through the generations, in Jesus' name. I am freed by the blood of Jesus. Let every void be filled now with Your love, Lord Jesus. Jesus, You are my victory. You are my liberty. You are my freedom. Oh, God, restore my soul, in Jesus' name. Amen."

Allow the Lord to restore to you your innocence as He cleanses you from all unrighteousness with His blood [1 John 1:9]. Purity is now the basis for your sexual union as a couple. Learn to become obedient to the voice of the Spirit. Jesus said the Holy Spirit would "guide us into all truth" [John 16:13], and that includes truth regarding intimacy in marriage. Ask God for the courage to obey. As you begin to approach sexual problems as one-flesh, you will begin to see healing emerge that you have not been able to attain on your own individually.

2. In the Bible, the Song of Solomon describes beautifully the intimate relationship between husband and wife. Within that text is found every element of sexual fulfillment as God has ordained it for marriage. If we study the verses, the depth of God's plan for sexual love is revealed to us.

Song of Solomon is graphically sensual. God is not bashful about His design for intimacy between husband and wife. In fact, the gratification of all five senses is found within the verses. The keys to the excitement of each of the senses give us a blueprint for the ingredients necessary for a healthy, vibrant sexual union.

Visual stimulation is an important aspect of sexual love [Song of Solomon 1:5; 4:1-7; 5:10-16]. A man is more sexually aroused by sight than a woman is. The devil has used this to great advantage in the world but God designed the man to respond favorably when he looks upon his wife. Both spouses need to realize that appearance is important, for though a wife is usually not stimulated visually, she may be hampered in her arousal by the unkempt appearance of her husband.

Become more aware of each other's appearance and ask God to remind you to show your admiration verbally. Be honest - start with something you truly admire, no matter how limited. As you move in obedience in this area, your appreciation and admiration will grow and deepen. Use this time to allow God to make you more aware of your own appearance. Is there anything you can do to be more appealing to your spouse? Do you need to lose weight? Get a haircut? Pay more attention to dress? Exercise? Brush your teeth more often? Ask the Lord to help you in any area of improvement in which He convicts you. Resolve today to be a blessing in your appearance to your spouse.

AREAS I RESOLVE TO WORK ON

HIM	HER
exercise	make up
dress up more	nails
hair - bald spot	exercise
	lose weight

Hearing is also part of sexual arousal [S. of S. 2:14b; 5:2; 7:8,9]. What we hear affects our perception of our spouse's feelings for us and often determines ours for them. Our words to each other have a bearing on our sexual union long before we enter into intimacy. Consistent words of endearment and praise will mean far more than words spoken just before anticipated love making.

God wants you to speak to each other regarding your appreciation for each other as sexual partners. Remember when you were first dating and how you admired each other? Has that appreciation gone out of your relationship? Do you as a husband realize and admire her beauty as you once did? Do you as a wife appreciate and admire his physique? We each need that so very much and yet sometimes it is the hardest thing for us to express to each other.

Read how the Lover and the Beloved speak to each other in Song of Solomon. Those two people had a true appreciation of each other and enjoyed a healthy physical relationship. They could openly express their love and desire for each other. That should be our goal also as husband and wife. Make a list of the things you appreciate about your spouse. Resolve to tell him or her often how you feel, not just when you want some desired result.

LIFE APPLICATION/WEEK 10 - INTIMACY

Lover to Beloved: (him to her)

Appreciate - allowing me to lead (even when I am not)
- *touching me (non-sexual)*
- *telling me you want me*
- *listening to me ... all the time, being a sounding board*
- *all the stuff you do for the kids*

Beautiful self, hair, nails (when you do them)

Beloved to Lover: (her to him)

Appreciate - love & support with our children
- *active participation in our family*
- *desire to help our family grow (spiritual & emotional)*
- *lead our family*

Handsome, dark hair and gorgeous blue eyes

    Smell [S. of S. 1:12; 4:10,11] and taste [S. of S. 2:3; 4:10, 11] are also important senses in sexual intimacy. We bless each other when we stimulate these senses with delightful fragrances. God does not make light of their affect on sexual intimacy, nor should we.

    Make sure your breath is fresh and clean. Toothpaste and mouthwashes leave a nice lingering taste. Experiment with different colognes and perfumes and see which ones you both like. Make use of testers in stores. Try burning scented candles or simmering potpourri while you are making love. Make the atmosphere soft and romantic, filled with delightful scents.

    Touch [S. of S. 1:2; 2:6; 8:3] is the final, not the first, step in sexual arousal. Stimulation of the other four senses will heighten the delight of sexual touch. Men need to be aware of the impact that this will have on sexual fulfillment for their wives. A woman is usually slower to arouse and will find more sexual fulfillment in a spouse who is willing to stimulate her other senses before proceeding to touch.

    Women especially love to be held, hugged, and kissed at times other than lovemaking. Tender holding on the part of a husband blesses and comforts a wife. The love and tenderness you show to her will be returned to you as she responds with greater and greater love [Ephesians 5:28].

3. Where your mind is during intercourse is very important. If you are thinking of someone else or imagining someone else, you are engaged in mental adultery. In the Song of Solomon both the lover and the beloved have their thoughts stayed on each other [Song of Solomon 7:10; 8:6,7], therefore, their desire for each other remains strong. Proverbs 23:7 (NKJV) says, *"For as he thinks in his heart, so is he..."* Our thought life determines our actions.

To deepen your sexual union, you need to concentrate on each other. Are either of you involved in pornography? Know for certain that there is no such thing as "innocent" pornography. Pornography comes from the same root word as "poneria" in Ephesians 6:12, which means depravity or spiritual wickedness. It is one of the most deceptive strongholds of the enemy. Lust is never satisfied. What is a thought today will be an action tomorrow. If the enemy cannot keep you from entering into the intimacy of God's covenant plan, marriage, he will attempt to make you compromise that covenant commitment. He tells you his counterfeits will bring excitement to your sexual union with your spouse but he knows they will rob you of intimacy with each other.

Do you read romance novels or watch soap operas? These things create a false image of sexual union. None of these give the image of lasting, maturing love. Each one portrays the excitement of lust at first sight and, as the excitement dies, the people involved must go on to other lovers to find the same excitement. God intends for our sexual union to grow and deepen just as our love for each other grows and deepens. If we are filling our minds with the world's garbage, we are going to seek after just that. But if we are filling our minds with the Word of God and asking Him for His plan for us, we will seek after that. Allow God to give you the sexual union He desires for you. It is so far above the imitation that the world has fabricated. Go for the very best God has to offer. It is well worth the effort it takes to achieve it.

Problems with pornography and lust cannot be overcome alone. You need the help of your spouse. First receive the deliverance and cleansing of the blood of Jesus. Then join together in one-flesh unity against these demonic strongholds. Become accountable to each other in areas of weakness. Remember, though, you are not your spouse's Holy Spirit. It is your job to intercede and to stand beside in support. Allow the conviction of sin to come from the One who does it best. The devil has used these tools to divide you in the past. Now join together in the power of Jesus against him and his forces of darkness. Together you will have the victory!

"Drink water from your own cistern, running water from your own well. Should your springs overflow in the streets, your streams of water in public places? Let them be yours alone, never to be shared with strangers. May your fountain be blessed, and may you rejoice in the wife of your youth. A loving doe, a graceful deer - may her breasts satisfy you always, may you ever be captivated by her love..." [Proverbs 5:15-20 NIV].

LIFE APPLICATION   WEEK 11 - SPIRITUAL WARFARE

1. Begin to see your home as a fort, fortified and protected against enemy attack. Think of some of the ways the enemy gains access inside that fort.

What can you do as a one-flesh team to prevent that entrance?

LIFE APPLICATION/WEEK 11 — SPIRITUAL WARFARE

2. As you remind yourselves daily that you are wearing the armor of God, use the following checklist to reinforce the purpose of each piece of equipment.

	MON	TUES	WED	THUR	FRI	SAT	SUN
HELMET							
BREASTPLATE							
BELT							
SHOES							
SWORD							
SHIELD							
PRAYER							

3. As part of your offensive warfare, once a week husband and wife should "patrol your hedge" and cover in prayer both the individual and family activities for the coming week. As you do that this week, record here what discernment the Holy Spirit gives you regarding enemy activity.

ACTIVITY	DISCERNMENT

How did you respond to the discernment of the Holy Spirit?

On the following pages you will find "incident reports" on which to record both offensive and defensive warfare encounters with the enemy. On each one record what the conflict involved; what enemy source you identified; and what action you took, including the weapons you used. This will aid you in keeping track of your spiritual warfare. Were you surprised by the attack? Did you have prior warning? Had the enemy attacked in this way before? Did you identify the hole in your hedge that allowed enemy entrance?

© Marriage Ministries International

LIFE APPLICATION/WEEK 11 — SPIRITUAL WARFARE

INCIDENT REPORT

DATE:

DESCRIPTION OF INCIDENT:

ENEMY IDENTIFIED:

ACTION TAKEN (INCLUDE DESCRIPTION OF WEAPONS USED):

WHAT YOU LEARNED AS A ONE-FLESH TEAM FROM THIS INCIDENT:

LIFE APPLICATION/WEEK 11 – SPIRITUAL WARFARE

INCIDENT REPORT

DATE:

DESCRIPTION OF INCIDENT:

ENEMY IDENTIFIED:

ACTION TAKEN (INCLUDE DESCRIPTION OF WEAPONS USED):

WHAT YOU LEARNED AS A ONE-FLESH TEAM FROM THIS INCIDENT:

LIFE APPLICATION   WEEK 12 - LIFE PATTERNS

*"Do not call to mind the former things,
or ponder things of the past.
Behold I will do something new
now it will spring forth.
Will you not be aware of it?
I will make even a roadway in the
wilderness, rivers in the desert."*
Isaiah 43:18,19

Ungodly life patterns create wildernesses and deserts in our marriages, areas that are dry and unfruitful. These are places where we have used the world's blueprint instead of the blueprint of the Word. God desires that something new spring forth in our lives. Through His Word He will make the roadway in the wilderness and the river in the desert of our marriage.

1. What are some life patterns the Holy Spirit has revealed to you that are operating in your own lives? Are they godly or ungodly? Give scripture to support your decision.

LIFE PATTERN	GODLY/UNGODLY	SCRIPTURE
Inconsistent time together	ungodly	Luke 12:31 *Seek ye first the*
Honest w/ each other *about sin*	godly	James 5:16
NOT Remember sabbath	ungodly	Matt 12:5 *Intent Rest + Worship*
		James 4:17

get better about praying for 1 another

training children

2. Now look at the life patterns that you have marked as ungodly. (If you don't have any, you're not being totally honest with yourselves.) What is God's pattern from His Word that would create a godly pattern for you? What would that godly pattern be?

SCRIPTURAL PATTERN FROM WORD	GODLY LIFE PATTERN CREATED
	Regular, daily time praying together & alone
	Rest + worship on the Sabbath

That's why I like Abeka

Not in ours Thank you God!

Does the actual day matter

© Marriage Ministries International

LIFE APPLICATION/WEEK 12 – LIFE PATTERNS

3. What changes are going to be necessary in your marriage to implement the godly pattern?

NEW GODLY PATTERN	CHANGES REQUIRED
Daily time praying	Rise earlier, get rest (bed earlier)
Rest & worship on Sabbath	Prepare ahead, be consistent

4. Are any of the ungodly life patterns present in relatives? Ask God to reveal to you if there are any generational influences in operation. If He shows you there are, take authority over them in Jesus' name.

> "Father, we thank you for showing us the generational patterns caused by these influences. We forgive any relatives who have wounded us because of these influences. We forgive each other for the times we have offended and hurt each other because of these influences. We release all who have offended us. Now in the mighty name of Jesus we take authority over the following generational influences. _daily devotion, observance of the Sabbath_ (write them in here and name them out loud). We cancel these influences over us and over our children and on down through the generations. We repent of having judged the actions of relatives under these influences. We repent for the ungodly patterns we have operated in under these influences and we receive Your forgiveness and the cleansing of the blood of Jesus. Teach us now from Your Word the godly pattern You would have us walk in. Amen."

5. Are there ungodly patterns that you see in your children that are a direct result of your actions? If so, share with them what you have learned and lead them in repentance. _Church attendence, daily time with God in prayer & studying his Word_

6. Now look at the godly patterns you have listed. (If you don't have any, you're not being totally honest with yourselves.) Praise the Lord that He has led you in these patterns, even if you have been unaware of it. What other godly patterns would you like to establish? What scriptures will guide you in these patterns?

LIFE APPLICATION/WEEK 12 – LIFE PATTERNS

7. If there is hidden sin in your life that you need to confess to your spouse, begin praying right now for the right timing in the Lord. This prayer need not be with your spouse right now. You should, however, give each other permission to confess sin as the Lord leads. Resolve right now to forgive when that sin is confessed. Set the stage for God to do a complete work between you, that there may be no darkness in your relationship. Then you can stand as Adam and Eve did, naked and unashamed before each other.

8. When one spouse confesses hidden sin to the other, take the necessary time for God to complete the healing. Allow the tears that are necessary for healing. Remember, Satan has already stolen from you and wounded your relationship. Don't give him further ground with strife and rejection of each other. Lock your shields together over the point of wounding and help protect each other against further attack. Do not let self-righteousness or self-pity take hold. This is a one-flesh problem—deal with it as such. Forgive each other as God has forgiven you. Do not place yourselves above God by refusing to forgive. Remember also that every sin has consequences for both spouses. Allow God to do a complete healing work in both of you. If hidden sexual sin has been confessed, go back to Lesson 10 and make sure you cover all that is necessary for freedom and healing.

9. Once hidden sin has been exposed and healing has begun, see this as an opportunity to begin again with a clean slate. Old sin is forgiven and forgotten. Start anew in Jesus, building new life patterns from His Word.

LIFE APPLICATION   WEEK 13 - ONE-FLESH MINISTRY

It is always good for us to realize how far God has brought us. Setting markers along our way helps us to remember where we were and appreciate where we are now. Record below how each of the thirteen weeks of your Married for Life group have ministered to specific areas of your marriage.

COVENANT _Commit to being married for life_

ONE-FLESH _See the two of us as one person working with God_

ROLES _how important what you say really is to your family_

SOWING AND REAPING _the results of what you do and don't do, what not acting on your call can do_

FORGIVENESS _the harm it can do not to, recognize when you need and how to_

FAITH VISION AND TRUST _time spent in the word will help us with this area_

PRAYING TOGETHER _Showed us the difference in can make and the peace it gives us, improve communication_

AGREEMENT _____

FLOWING TOGETHER IN THE SPIRIT _____

INTIMACY _____

SPIRITUAL WARFARE _____

© Marriage Ministries International

LIFE APPLICATION/WEEK 13 — ONE-FLESH MINISTRY

LIFE PATTERNS _help to see some of the good ones and gave encouragement to change the bad ones_

ONE-FLESH MINISTRY _helps to determine what season we are in and move forward_

1. Which areas are the most difficult for you and present the greatest challenge for improvement? _All of them — different time we struggle with them all._

What are you doing to work on these areas as one-flesh?

Trying to apply what we have learned.

2. Discuss as a couple what season you believe you are in now. In your own personal walk with the Lord you may vary in growth and development but this question is regarding you as a one-flesh team. Are you still in a season of self-focus and primarily receiving or have you moved into the third season? If you are in the first or second season, how do you see God using what you are now receiving?

Season Two. Open our eyes and strengthen what we have, our family.

If you have entered into the third season, how are you now sowing and reaping and planting vineyards?

LIFE APPLICATION/WEEK 13 — ONE-FLESH MINISTRY

3. In order to consistently move forward in our one-flesh relationship we need to set specific goals and work toward them. Without goals we have no way of measuring our progress. Someone once said, "If you aim for nothing, you will probably hit it." In the remainder of this homework, set two personal goals (two each for husband and wife), two one-flesh goals, and two goals related to your call as one-flesh. Following each goal set a one-month, three-month, six-month, and nine-month objective that will help you meet that goal in one year's time. By meeting short-term objectives, the goals will be accomplished on a timely basis.

Personal goals (Wife)
Goal 1: _Be a better administrator of our house_

Goal 2: _Change the home atmosphere_

Personal goals (Husband)
Goal 1: _Be a better Provider (Spiritual) to my family._

Goal 2: _Be a better leader for my family_

Now state what you will do by one month from now, three months from now, six months from now, and nine months from now to meet each of these goals.

Wife
Goal 1: _Admin_
One month _Clear up clutter around house_

Three months _Have homeschool prep done for the year and school started._
Six months _Money situation straightened out._

Nine months _____

Goal 2: _Home Atmosphere_
One month _Speak good about husband + children to them and others_
Three months _Keep this calm by not overscheduling in the fall_
Six months _Have the children help make Christmas gifts to give_

Nine months _____

LIFE APPLICATION/WEEK 13 – ONE-FLESH MINISTRY

Husband
Goal 1: Spiritual Provider
One month start weekly family meeting, nightly prays again
Three months memorize scripture

Six months start planning quarterly service project for family
Nine months have children reading and telling us (and others) about Bible stories
Goal 2: Leader
One month pray daily in the morning before I start my day
Three months Lead by example the changes that I want family to do.
Six months Have more control over my emotions

Nine months _____

One-flesh
Goal 1: _____

One month _____

Three months _____

Six months _____

Nine months _____

Goal 2: _____

One month _____

Three months _____

Six months _____

LIFE APPLICATION/WEEK 13 — ONE-FLESH MINISTRY

Nine months _____
_____

Goals related to your call
Goal 1: _____
_____

One month _____
_____

Three months _____
_____

Six months _____
_____

Nine months _____
_____

Goal 2: _____
_____

One month _____
_____

Three months _____
_____

Six months _____
_____

Nine months _____
_____

Be diligent in meeting these goals. All of us need structure in which to grow. Let this be your guideline as the Spirit leads you on in your growth together. Remember, this is just the beginning of the rest of your life together. Allow Jesus to work in you and through you to make the very most of it.

WHAT GOD CAN GET THROUGH YOU, HE'LL GET TO YOU.

Couples In Our Group

Name: Dave + Chris Stark
Address: 1248 Canvasback Dr.
Aubrey, TX 76227
Phone: 972/347-3412

Name: David + ~~Sophie~~ Safeeya Schnaufer
Address: 3122 Barton Rd.
Carrollton, TX 75007
Phone: 972/394-4686

Name: Gene + Kathleen Ruble
Address: 3812 Pecan Crossing
The Colony, TX 75056
Phone: Home 972/370-3600
B 972/896-1300

Name: Cliff + Kathy Smith
Address: 3828 Westminster
Carrollton, TX 75007
Phone: 972/394-9420

Name: Giles + Connie Hudson
Address: 972/625-5941
Phone: 97

Name:
Address:
Phone:

Name:
Address:
Phone:

LIFE APPLICATION/WEEK 13 – ONE-FLESH MINISTRY

OUR OUTREACH NIGHT

DATE:

LOCATION:

TIME:

OUR ASSIGNMENT:

PEOPLE WE ARE GOING TO INVITE:

NAME:	DATE INVITED

Ministry Opportunities with Marriage Ministries International

There are as many one-flesh calls of God as there are couples. God has just the right one for you and we wish you His greatest blessing as you pursue it. We pray that your third season will be fruitful to the glory of God!

For those who are led of the Lord to minister to marriages, Marriage Ministries International leadership offers many ministry opportunities. You may be called of God to lead a Married for Life group, teaching and ministering directly to couples. Or, if you have administrative skills, office skills, artistic talent, or just enjoy contact with people, God may be leading you into the valuable ministry of helps. If you cannot give of your time and talents to the ministry and still desire to bless MMI, you may opt to become an Alumni Giver. A description of ministry opportunities within Marriage Ministries International is contained in the following text. If you feel called in any one of these areas, please send in the sheet at the end of this lesson. A staff member in your area will contact you.

REMEMBER—GOD HAS GIVEN YOU MUCH AND BLESSED YOU MIGHTILY THAT YOU MIGHT REACH OUT IN HIS NAME AND BLESS OTHERS [Luke 12:48; Matthew 10:8].

MARRIED FOR LIFE GROUP LEADERSHIP

OBJECTIVES OF THE MINISTRY

The vision and purpose of Marriage Ministries International is to equip couples to walk in the fullness of their one-flesh relationship so that they may fulfill the call of God on their lives. The scriptural principles shared weekly for thirteen weeks teach couples how to walk in the power of the Spirit, making their home an oasis of peace to their neighborhood and community. They become a powerhouse Christian home that knows how to minister salvation, deliverance, and healing in the name of Jesus. The strength, unity, and synergistic power that flows from their one-flesh relationship is used mightily of the Lord to minister to others.

HOW COUPLES MINISTER

Group Leaders are responsible for teaching the weekly lessons, training the Leaders in Training, and ministering to couples in their groups. Leadership in Marriage Ministries International requires that a couple be operating in one-flesh scriptural principles in their own life and be willing to share them with others. Couples qualifying for leadership must be born-again and Spirit-filled with evidence of speaking in tongues.

Leaders in Training spend the thirteen weeks learning to lead an Married for Life group of their own. BECOMING A LEADER IN TRAINING SIGNIFIES THE INTENT TO BECOME MMI LEADERSHIP.

WHAT IS EXPECTED OF MMI LEADERSHIP

Marriage Ministries International leadership must have a heart for God's best for marriages and must realize they are entering into a ministry called of God. MMI leadership is a year-round ministry just the same as any ministry within the Church. Group Leaders are expected to lead Married for Life groups after training. Along with teaching the weekly classes, Group Leaders need to meet weekly with their Leaders in Training to intercede for their group. They must also be available for the couples in their group as necessary. They are also required to attend periodic leadership meetings and training sessions. Prerequisites for leadership are: both spouses are born-again and Spirit-filled with evidence of speaking in tongues, attendance at an MMI group as a member couple or completion of a training weekend, a recommendation from their pastor, completion of a leadership questionnaire, and approval by city or area leadership.

TRAINING

Training for MMI leadership is accomplished as Leaders in Training on the job with a Group Leader for the thirteen week group. All requirements for leadership must be met by the assistant couple before they can be approved to lead a Married for Life group of their own.

In areas where no Married for Life groups are presently meeting, leadership training is accomplished in a weekend training session running from Friday morning to Sunday afternoon.

MARRIAGE MINISTRIES INTERNATIONAL HELPS MINISTRIES

HOW COUPLES MINISTER

Each city, area, state, or regional leadership couple in Marriage Ministries International has great need for couples who will assist them in administrative areas. Office skills such as typing and filing are a constant area of need. Couples are also needed to place follow-up phone calls, assist in securing meeting places, and community contacts. Transportation and delivery of supplies is a ministry opportunity also available. Those with artistic talent, printing and typesetting ability, writing skills, photography skills, editing ability, etc. are needed in times of projects requiring those abilities. People with a flare for decorating can provide valuable assistance.

Intercessors are needed both for leadership couples and for the ministry. People desiring to minister to children can be a blessing during MMI public meetings and leadership meetings. Those given to hospitality can be a blessing organizing picnics and other get-togethers.

HOW COUPLES MINISTER

Couples called to minister in MMI in these areas will directly assist the city, area, state or regional leaders who have requested the help on an "as needed" basis. As Marriage Ministries International grows in size and scope, each city will have permanent administrative personnel who will oversee these functions.

© Marriage Ministries International

LIFE APPLICATION/WEEK 13 — ONE-FLESH MINISTRY

TRAINING

Since most couples volunteering for this type of ministry bring their own skills, the majority of training will concentrate on familiarizing volunteers with the needs of Marriage Ministries International.

ALUMNI GIVERS

The ongoing financial support of this ministry is vital to its strengthening and growth. Marriage Ministries International relies on the generosity of couples who have been blessed through MMI. Those who have been most blessed are the ones who give most to help others be reached. Consistent financial support from Married for Life Alumni helps provide steady finances throughout the year for ongoing salaries and office maintenance here in the U.S. and for expansion and growth throughout the world into other nations.

If you have been blessed by the ministry of Marriage Ministries International and feel God speaking to you to be an ongoing financial supporter, you can be assured that the finances given into this ministry are prayerfully used to support and maintain existing MMI ministry and to expand into new areas of ministry as God directs. Becoming an Alumni Giver puts you in the company of couples all over the world who have a heart to reach the homes of the nations with God's blueprint for marriages. Alumni Givers receive special discounts and gifts and are kept current regarding the finances of this ministry through periodic financial statements.

If you believe God is leading you into one or more of these areas of ministry, please complete the ministry application form in your packet and give it to your Group Leaders or mail it to the National Office.

AND REMEMBER, THIS IS NOT THE END. IT IS ONLY THE BEGINNING OF THE REST OF YOUR MARRIAGE. WHAT YOU MAKE OF IT DEPENDS ON HOW WILLING YOU ARE TO BE OBEDIENT TO THE LORD AND HIS WORD. DO THE HOMEWORK THIS WEEK TOGETHER AND SEEK HIM REGARDING YOUR NEXT STEPS.